THE
ANCESTRAL
TABLE

TRADITIONAL RECIPES FOR A PALEO LIFESTYLE

by

RUSS CRANDALL

PHOTOGRAPHED BY GIANG CAO AND RUSS CRANDALL

ILLUSTRATIONS BY ALEX BOAKE

VICTORY BELT PUBLISHING INC.
Las Vegas

First Published in 2013 by Victory Belt Publishing Inc.

Copyright © Russ Crandall

ISBN 13: 978-1-628600-05-6

Printed in the USA

RRD 0113

CONTENTS

Bear in mind that you should conduct yourself in life as at a feast.
-EPICTETUS

FOREWORD

© PerfectHealthDiet.com

How should we eat?

Russ Crandall has an answer: *gourmet ancestral cuisine*. We should eat as if we were gourmet chefs of the Paleolithic era—the caveman's Julia Child or Anthony Bourdain.

Pairing gourmet and ancestral sounds odd, as unlikely as Mammoth Bourguignon, Dodo St. Jacques, or Sabertooth Provençale. Gourmet cuisine, after all, is a recent invention. Only a few hundred years ago, spices like pepper, saffron, cinnamon, and nutmeg were so rare and precious that Europeans valued them above gold. Sugar, so abundant and cheap today, was considered a medicine, not a food, and the word itself was coined only in the 13th century; crusader William of Tyre had called it "sweet salt." Without modern wealth and transportation technologies to bring ingredients from all over the world, it seems, there could not have been anything resembling gourmet cuisine.

Even if we *can* unite gourmet and Paleolithic cuisine, why should we? Popular wisdom holds that, as Mark Twain said, "The only way to keep your health is to eat what you don't want, drink what you don't like, and do what you'd rather not." Wouldn't eating gourmet food every day wreck our health?

But the science says Twain was wrong and Russ is right. Both the cavemen and the gourmands have important things to teach us about healthful eating.

Let me introduce myself. My name is Paul Jaminet, and I am, with my wife Shou-Ching, the author of *Perfect Health Diet: Regain Health and Lose Weight by Eating the Way You Were Meant to Eat,* published by Scribner in 2012.

Shou-Ching and I invented the Perfect Health Diet, or PHD, as our readers like to call it, as a cure for our personal health problems. Our journey to the PHD began in 2005 when we first tried the Paleo diet—a popular approximation of Paleolithic diets. At the time we both had chronic diseases that had gotten worse every year for a dozen years, with no help from doctors. The Paleo diet was the first thing we tried that made a difference. The differences were both good and bad—some things got better, some things got worse—but we were excited because we had found a tool that could change the course of our diseases.

Hippocrates was on to something when he said, "Let food be thy medicine." *Diet matters for health,* and a good diet has great healing power.

We adopted a research strategy for finding the perfect diet. Starting from an ancestral template—meaning we'd eat only natural whole foods, the kinds that our ancestors hunted and gathered—we would avoid any food that contained significant amounts of toxins after cooking. To find the right proportions of different food types, we researched the optimal intake level of every nutrient and designed the diet to include foods in specific proportions that deliver the optimal amount of every nutrient simultaneously—assuring neither a deficiency nor an excess of any nutrient.

It took us seven years of research to design this diet. When we were done, we were shocked to find that it bore a remarkable resemblance to gourmet cuisine. Our food was delicious!

We soon realized that this was no coincidence. Why did a taste preference for certain foods and food combinations evolve in human beings? To give us heart attacks? Surely not: evolution favors those who succeed, who are healthy and fit and survive to have children and grandchildren.

Evolution must have designed our taste preferences to make us healthy. In our ancestral environment—the environment of the Paleolithic era—eating delicious gourmet-style food must have been the path to great health. It must have generated virile warriors, productive hunters and gatherers, insightful toolmakers, and fertile mothers and fathers.

Nor were our Paleolithic ancestors unable to design complex meals that appealed to those innate taste preferences. Cooking is as ancient as the control of fire: anthropologist Richard Wrangham argues that cooking may have been invented as early as 1.6 million years ago. Animal hides over an open flame will not burn as long as they contain water, and they make fine stew and soup pots. Communal feasts were probably common by about 250,000 years ago, when hearths became common features of human dwellings. Paleolithic chefs undoubtedly had many ingredients to choose from: they were intimately familiar with their plant and animal environment, and anthropologists find residues of hundreds of food species in individual Paleolithic settlements—far more variety than the thirty or so species that most modern Americans eat.

With the development of agriculture and civilization, kitchen technologies progressed and the range of cooking methods broadened; transportation improvements enabled the gathering of ingredients and recipe ideas from all over the world; and increasing numbers of chefs, supported by wealthy clients, acquired the time and resources to refine recipes. Simple Paleolithic cooking methods were made sophisticated, and the world's traditional cuisines developed. Recipes were continually refined to become ever more satisfying.

Caveman cooking became traditional cuisine; traditional cuisines turned into gourmet artistry.

We stand at a pivotal moment in the history of food. Two threads of insight are now ready for a synthesis. On one hand, we appreciate more than ever that our innate taste preferences are our friends. We should eat to please ourselves, for it is gourmet food that will bring us good health. On the other hand, we realize that those taste preferences can mislead us if we try to satisfy them with unnatural ingredients. Many agricultural and industrial ingredients, some developed recently in chemistry laboratories, appeal to our innate taste preferences even as they fail to nourish our bodies. Our path to good health is clear. We must reproduce our ancestral food environment today by confining ourselves to the natural whole foods and gentle cooking methods available to our Paleolithic ancestors. With that restriction in place, our taste preferences will guide us.

It's not necessary to master the science of nutrition in order to be healthy. It is necessary to be able to cook delicious food. You must be able to combine ingredients in delectable ways. That's what Russ and *The Ancestral Table* are here to teach us. Drawing upon the world's traditional cuisines and their accumulated knowledge of the most delicious food combinations, Russ shows us how to make the world's most healthful food.

So what is the optimal balance of foods, the proportions that supply optimal nutrition?

We represent the optimal proportions in our PHD food plate in the shape of a yin-yang apple:

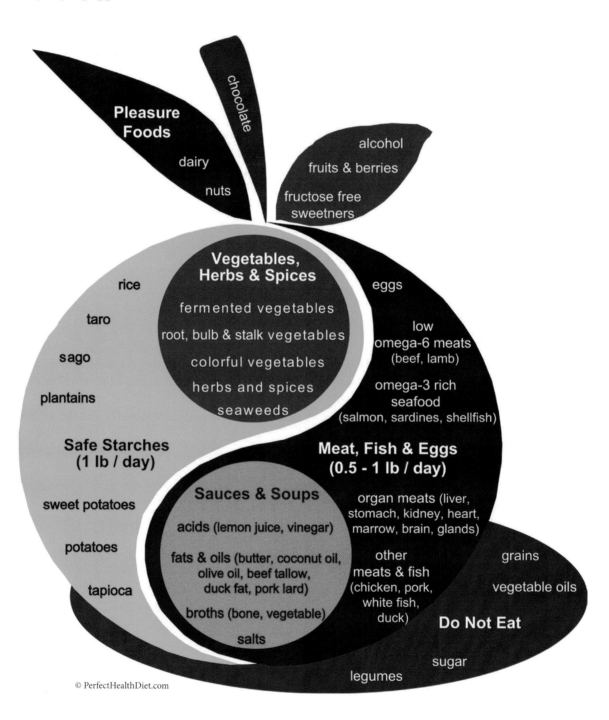

Pleasure Foods

chocolate

dairy

nuts

alcohol

fruits & berries

fructose free sweetners

Vegetables, Herbs & Spices

fermented vegetables

root, bulb & stalk vegetables

colorful vegetables

herbs and spices

seaweeds

eggs

low omega-6 meats (beef, lamb)

omega-3 rich seafood (salmon, sardines, shellfish)

rice

taro

sago

plantains

Safe Starches (1 lb / day)

sweet potatoes

potatoes

tapioca

Meat, Fish & Eggs (0.5 - 1 lb / day)

Sauces & Soups

acids (lemon juice, vinegar)

fats & oils (butter, coconut oil, olive oil, beef tallow, duck fat, pork lard)

broths (bone, vegetable)

salts

organ meats (liver, stomach, kidney, heart, marrow, brain, glands)

other meats & fish (chicken, pork, white fish, duck)

grains

vegetable oils

Do Not Eat

sugar

legumes

© PerfectHealthDiet.com

The body of the apple represents the components of a meal; the yin-yang symbol represents a balance of plant and animal foods. The leaves and stem represent pleasure foods that should be eaten in moderation. In the shadow of the apple are foods to avoid—cereal grains, sugar, beans and peanuts, and vegetable seed oils.

A DAY'S MEALS SHOULD INCLUDE THE FOLLOWING:

- About a pound of "safe starches"—starchy plants that are low in toxins after cooking, such as white rice and potatoes
- About a pound, or a bit less, of meat, fish, and eggs—the complementary animal foods to the starches
- A diversity of fruits and vegetables, adding up to several pounds a day or so, to complement the starches and provide healthful fiber and nutrition
- Flavorful sauces composed of healthy fats, such as butter, beef fat, olive oil, avocado, coconut oil, and macadamia nut butter; acids, such as vinegar, citric acid from lemons or other citrus fruits, and lactic acid from fermented vegetables; and umami flavors, such as those found in fermented foods

It is good to combine all four of these types of foods in every meal. Doing so not only adds complexity and flavor, but also renders the food more digestible and helps the body metabolize the meal properly.

One last step to healthful eating is to make certain highly nourishing foods a regular part of your diet. We call them *supplemental foods* because they supply key nutrients that are hard to obtain from other sources and should be eaten regularly, like supplements.

Our supplemental foods, so crucial for good health, include egg yolks (you can eat the whites, too, but the yolks have the crucial nutrients); collagen-rich soups and stews made from simmering bones, joints, and tendons; liver and other organ meats; diverse vegetables; shellfish and oily seafood; fermented foods such as kimchi, yogurt, and aged cheese; and, believe it or not, dark chocolate.

My wife and I began eating "gourmet ancestral cuisine" because of our health problems. For Russ, too, poor health was the inspiration for a delicious diet. Russ had a stroke at age 24—a shocking event for a seemingly healthy man—and then discovered he had a life-threatening autoimmune disease, Takayasu's arteritis. Russ's health problems receded after he adopted an ancestral diet, as they did for my wife and me.

Experiences like Russ's and ours are terrific motivation for cooking great meals. We know we need this delicious food!

But for a healthy person, it's tempting to take an easier path. And that's what most people do: they eat whatever is readily available, no matter how poor the quality.

That tendency to chow down on whatever food is closest at hand—even if it is as malnourishing as cookies and soda—frustrates diet experts to no end. So powerful is the impulse to minimize time and effort in food acquisition that people eat more or less the same diet all over the world. In nearly every country, two-thirds or more of calories come from the staple agricultural crops that the PHD mostly forbids: cereal grains, beans, sugar, and vegetable seed oils.

As more and more food consumption has shifted to industrially produced foods made from the cheapest, least nourishing, and most toxic ingredients, it's no surprise that health is becoming impaired. Rates of obesity, diabetes, and auto-immune diseases are rising, and there is reason to believe that life expectancy itself may soon peak and then start to decline.

The temptation to eat what is readily available instead of what is healthful, to buy food prepared in a factory rather than cook for oneself and one's family—this is a temptation that should be resisted. The effects of industrial food are insidious and hard to notice at first, but over decades they build up, damage health, and shorten life spans.

In *The Ancestral Table,* Russ has assembled the information you need to set yourself and your family on a different path. He integrates the delicious recipe ideas of traditional cuisines, refined over centuries, with the healthful ingredients of our ancestors. Follow the path of gourmet ancestral cuisine. Learn the pleasures of cooking—let the odors of a gourmet meal simmering on the stove pervade your home. It will bring you joy today and good health tomorrow.

And when, as a centenarian, you look back on a lifetime of delicious home-cooked food, don't forget to remind your great-grandchildren that good health comes from an ancestral table!

—PAUL JAMINET, PHD

INTRODUCTION

My journey toward creating this book has been an interesting one, so let me walk you through it.

Life as a Kid

I spent my childhood in a turn-of-the-century farmhouse in Port Orchard, Washington, with three brothers and a baby sister. My appreciation for food started early; my nickname as a toddler was "the vacuum cleaner," for obvious reasons. I remember most of my childhood being led stomach-first: foraging for wild berries and fruits in our small orchard, swiping tubs of cake frosting from the pantry, and having a battle of wills with my mom over the merits of onions in cooking (she had two arguments—"I cut them up small so you won't notice them" or "I cut them up big so you can pick them out easily"). When I was a teenager, we moved to a small town nestled in the foothills of Mount Rainier—Yelm, Washington—where I lived until I graduated from high school.

My Culinary Journey Begins

My first job was at a fast-food burger chain, but I soon branched out and tried my hand as a chef at a local pizza parlor and a couple full-service restaurants. Until I was able to pay for my own meals, I ate home-cooked meals almost exclusively. My palate quickly expanded as I started to try new foods. I discovered other cuisines and started developing confidence in my own talents as a chef.

At age 20, I needed to make a decision: continue working as a chef and slowly crawl through college, or try a whole new path. So I joined the United States Navy and was promptly shipped off to basic training. I signed on as a Russian translator and spent a couple years learning the language before moving to my first duty station near Pearl Harbor on the Hawaiian island of O'ahu. During my seven years in Hawaii, I spent most of my time traveling and deploying onboard Navy warships, providing language support at sea.

I could go on and on about my many adventures traveling the Pacific and picking up another language—Indonesian—along the way. But some of the most relevant facts regarding my time in Hawaii are these: I had a unique opportunity to travel the world, experience new cultures, and try new cuisines. I also met my wife, Janey, and had a few health-related hiccups.

A Curious Decline in Health

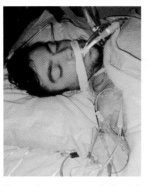

In 2005, at age 24, I had a stroke. Up until this point I had been a model of health: I exercised regularly, lived an active lifestyle, and tried my best to eat a diet aligned with the food pyramid. And then I woke up one morning and the left side of my body wasn't working properly. The doctors who treated me determined that the stroke was the result of a lesion (most likely a blood clot) on the right side of my pons, a part of the brain stem. This explained the loss of fine motor function on my left side, but no one could figure out what had actually caused the stroke. It took me a few months of therapy, but my young brain quickly recovered, and I relearned how to walk, write, and hold a fork.

A year later, I found myself having a hard time catching my breath while exercising. I had difficulty jogging, let alone running, and despite intense effort to get back into shape, I just couldn't pull together the energy to do it. Eventually I couldn't even walk without getting winded, and I decided to see a doctor. I spent the next month living in hospitals, undergoing every test I'd seen on TV's *House.* The doctors finally settled on the idea that my pulmonary arteries were experiencing some sort of blockage, which they later figured out was caused by inflammation.

I was diagnosed with Takayasu's arteritis, a rare autoimmune disease that causes inflammation and narrowing of arteries. My case was especially strange because Takayasu's arteritis occurs predominantly in women of Asian heritage (strikes one and two) and only rarely in the pulmonary arteries (strike three). As with most autoimmune diseases, the cause of Takayasu's arteritis is not known.

Playing the Modern Medical Game

I spent a year on heavy drug therapy—a combination of steroids and other immunosuppressants. While they allowed me to function, I wasn't happy with the idea of spending the rest of my life tethered to drug therapy that could potentially cause health issues for me later in life. So in 2007 I elected to have a pulmonary resectioning surgery performed at a major pulmonary institute in California. During the ten-hour procedure, I was put into full cardiac arrest using deep hypothermia and a full cardiopulmonary bypass. In other words, the doctors cooled my body to stop blood circulation and kept me in a state of hibernation, with a machine taking over my heart and lung functions; I was clinically dead for eight hours. The surgeons removed inflamed tissue from my pulmonary arteries and reconstructed the arteries using cow parts.

As you might imagine, this procedure is tricky, and only a few places in the world do it. It carries a high mortality rate due to its inherent complications. I'm happy to say that I made it out okay. It was definitely one of the hardest and most painful moments of my life, but even more painful was the fact that the surgery didn't ease my symptoms. After gambling with my life and hoping it would fix my ailments, I was on the same amount of medication and felt no significant improvement in my pulmonary performance.

Bear in mind that through all this, life still went on—I got married a few months before the surgery and even went on a deployment between health crises. Without the support of my wife, family, friends, and military family, I'm not sure I could have made it through this crazy time.

Taking Matters into My Own Hands

Years went by. Janey and I moved to the Baltimore area in 2008 and welcomed our son, Oliver, into the world in 2009. I continued to work as a translator in the Navy. The heavy medication was taking its toll, especially the steroids. I was nearly 40 pounds over my normal weight, my bones were becoming progressively more brittle, and I couldn't build muscle to save my life. I was becoming increasingly tired all the time and was experiencing health events that were simply not normal for my age—I had a painful bout of shingles due to my compromised immune system, and I was having trouble remembering simple things, which is often associated with steroid therapy.

And then in 2010 I came across a blog post that mentioned the Paleo diet. It was shown to reverse instances of cardiovascular disease, diabetes, and autoimmune symptoms. Within a week I had thrown out all the garbage in our pantry and started eating whole foods and meals based on ancestral principles. I immediately felt better. My inflammation markers improved so dramatically in that first month that I convinced my doctors to decrease my immunosuppressant medication, and I was off steroid therapy quickly thereafter.

I dropped those extra 40 pounds nearly overnight, and everything went back to normal, or at least closer to normal than I had been in many years. I simply started feeling like I did before getting sick. Over the course of the next few years, I was able to wean myself off every medication but one, when at my worst I had been taking more than a dozen pills a day and self-injecting medications into my stomach.

I'll be the first person to say that changing my diet didn't completely cure me—there's no mistaking the fact that I still have a serious and debilitating autoimmune condition—but I can say with confidence that changing my diet improved my health by leaps and bounds.

Sharing My Story

I started my blog, *The Domestic Man,* several months before switching my diet. I opened the website with the idea that we humans have become domesticated, that we have lost touch with our lineage. Many cultures have stopped passing down traditions from one generation to the next, one of the most important traditions being how we gather and prepare our meals. Today, an alarming number of Americans don't know where our food comes from or how to prepare food beyond taking it out of a box and heating it up.

So I decided to reconnect with nature by chronicling my cooking adventures. Once I started trying to write recipes that were in line with my new way of eating, I discovered a trend: there are a ton of delicious, healthy dishes to be found nestled in the pages of history. So I adjusted my website to focus on fundamental, traditional dishes that are historically relevant. Along the way I also realized that gourmet cuisine rests on the foundation of traditional foods and is quite possibly the ideal culmination of history and science. And the main idea of this cookbook was born.

This book is the result of several years' worth of research and experimentation, my attempt to compile a collection of dishes that are based on traditional recipes (both relatively new and ancient) found all over the world. If human beings have been eating this way since antiquity, why switch things up now?

CHAPTER 1

DIET AND KITCHEN FUNDAMENTALS

The Paleo Template

I'd like to take a second to go over the basis of the Paleo diet for anyone who's new to the concept.

The Paleo (short for Paleolithic) diet is based on the ancestral human diet. It focuses on whole foods like meats, vegetables, and fruits while avoiding foods that are problematic to many people's digestive systems. The Paleo diet is not a reenactment of prehistoric diets; it uses scientific study and evolutionary evidence to figure out the optimal diet for our modern age.

The Paleo diet is not the first attempt at restoring an ancestrally minded lifestyle. In the late 19th century, a movement known as the Physical Culture Movement sprang up as a reaction to increasingly sedentary lifestyles of post–Industrial Revolution society. Followers of the movement avoided what they considered "diseases of affluence" by eating natural foods, increasing exposure to air, bathing in rivers, and getting plenty of sunshine.

Weston A. Price was a dentist who found a relationship between dental health and nutrition; in researching for his 1939 book, *Nutrition and Physical Degeneration: A Comparison of Primitive and Modern Diets and Their Effects,* Price studied many pre-industrial populations around the world and found that those eating indigenous diets were free of diseases that had become typical in the West. His work is the basis of the Western A. Price Foundation, one of the largest whole-foods and traditional movements today.

In 1975, gastroenterologist Walter L. Voetlin published a book called *The Stone Age Diet,* which concludes that humans are primarily carnivores by nature, with some allowance for carbohydrates. Since the 1980s, several doctors, nutritionists, and scholars have published works asserting that a diet based on ancestral principles is ideal for modern societies. Loren Cordain, a professor at Colorado State University, first published *The Paleo Diet* in 2001, and it became the basis for our modern interpretation of the diet, focusing on meats and vegetables. Robb Wolf published *The Paleo Solution* in 2010, which refined Cordain's principles and attracted mainstream attention and popularity.

Today, several versions of the Paleo diet exist. Dallas and Melissa Hartwig's Whole30 program (outlined in their book *It Starts with Food*) provides a tough-love plan to transform your diet through their 30-day reset, which follows strict Paleo guidelines. Mark Sisson's *The Primal Blueprint* is consistent with most Paleo principles but is more lenient with dairy and alcohol. In the Foreword to this book, Paul Jaminet describes his Perfect Health Diet, which advocates moderate consumption of safe starches in ratios that are aligned with those found in indigenous diets worldwide. The Perfect Health Diet is the diet that I follow and demonstrate in this book; indeed, you could call this the first Perfect Health Diet cookbook.

My Dietary and Culinary Tenets

As you'll see in later sections, I support a historically minded way of eating that is delicious, sustainable, and based on Paleo diet principles. The concept of dieting is both foreign and unnatural to how humans have lived for all of history. Instead, I believe that the way we eat should be a healthy combination of traditional practices and informed research to find what works for us as individuals.

Guiding principles

In this modern world of processed, hyper-palatable (and, admittedly, delicious) Frankenfoods, I find that the key to maintaining a healthy diet is to focus on tasty, nutrient-rich foods. The foundation of this book rests on the idea that throughout history, humankind has been cooking with taste—not health—in mind, and that our natural taste preferences are actually tuned in to what is most healthful; that's why our preferences evolved in the first place. In other words, there's a reason we crave fatty, salty foods—it's because they are good for us (assuming that they come from natural whole-food sources).

With this book I hope to satisfy your innate food preferences while guiding you to better health. Here are the principles I use to guide my recipe development:

1 **Nutrient-rich and low-toxicity foods.** Foods should be nourishing and support a healthy gut. Foods from happy, naturally raised animals are important. Fermented foods and bone broths should be daily meal staples, and other nutrient-rich foods, like egg yolks, organ meats, and seafood, should be consumed frequently. These ingredients are heavily represented in this cookbook, but in reality I've shown only the tip of the iceberg. Meals should be free of major toxins, like those found in most cereal grains, legumes, and processed foods (see "Prioritizing your food choices" on page 23).

2 **Ideal macronutrient ratio.** I like to think in terms of plant foods versus animal foods, and I try to portion my plate to be three-quarters plant foods and one-quarter animal foods: one meat, one starch, and two vegetable sides. My two vegetable sides tend to be a hearty vegetable (carrots, broccoli) and a leafy vegetable (salad). Macronutrient (carbs/proteins/fats) ratios are highly individualized, but a ratio of 50% fats, 30% proteins, and 20% carbs is a good general figure. If you are looking to lose weight, I would suggest lowering your carbohydrate intake and increase your fat intake as appropriate. I have kept portion sizes purposely vague in this book so that you can build your meals to fit your own health goals.

3 **Historically appropriate dishes.** Many traditional and international foods are naturally gluten-free and Paleo-friendly and have been developed and perfected over hundreds of years. I prefer to make these dishes with minimal tweaks instead of re-creating them using offbeat ingredient substitutions. I also support gentle cooking methods akin to those that were historically

available; you'll find a lot of recipes that involve simmering and roasting at low temperatures.

4 **Natural umami flavors.** I use a heavy amount of natural flavor enhancers like broths, tomatoes, seafood, fermented foods, and acids to make dishes tasty. This has been done throughout history. Combining fats, acids, and starches is a common culinary practice, and a lot of evidence suggests that this combination aids in digestion and nutrient absorption.

5 **A variety of plant parts.** Our ancestors often ate every edible part of any plant they could find and used a variety of cooking techniques to keep dishes interesting. We should do the same. Not to mention that if we ate only leafy greens or carrots all the time, we'd go crazy. In general, plants can be divided into seven main sections: tubers (potatoes), bulbs (onions, garlic), roots (carrots, parsnips, turnips), stems (asparagus, celery), leaves (cabbage, lettuce), flowers (broccoli, cauliflower, artichokes), and fruits (tomatoes, cucumbers, eggplant, squash). Botanically, tubers, bulbs, and roots are all considered roots, but you get my point. I make sure to eat a variety of plant parts each week. Eating a variety of fungi (mushrooms) is also ideal.

6 **No shortcuts.** It's a hard truth to face, but if you're too busy to properly cook a meal, you may want to find out what's making you so busy and reprioritize. There are several reasons for my belief that cooking is a challenge that should be faced head-on. First and foremost, cooking is a beautiful art that anyone can enjoy, and it's something that mankind has embraced for thousands of years. Truly understanding how your food is prepared provides immense satisfaction. Next, foods often are at their most delicious when cooked for extended periods, as evidenced by the fact that many of the most delicious meals out there require a significant investment of time. They're also often more nutritious—a bone broth cooked for ten hours, for example, is more nutrient-dense than a broth cooked for one hour. Finally, cooking is a skill that's been passed down from generation to generation since the dawn of humankind. Somehow we've lost this tradition over the past 100 years. It's time to take it back.

Environmental factors

I believe that our rise in food intolerances and allergies are the result of our modern environment. Today, we are more susceptible to and affected by problematic foods because we're not connected to nature in the same ways humans have been throughout history.

Plenty of access to the great outdoors, constant contact with livestock, and the consumption of a wide variety of fresh, seasonal, and naturally fermented foods were all staples of the human condition until our modern era. We've further weakened our gut flora (the bacteria that helps us digest foods and absorb nutrients) by misusing antibiotics and overusing antibacterial products, which kill off both good and bad bacteria. The foods we eat today are less nutritious due to soil depletion and negligent mass-farming practices. We don't get enough sleep, and we live in a constant state of low-level stress. These factors contribute to a weakened system and an increase in food allergies and autoimmune-related health issues.

Prioritizing your food choices

If I had to put foods into categories, I'd have three: Good, Great, and Bad. You should eat mostly Good foods, supplement with Great foods as much as possible, and avoid Bad foods.

GOOD: MEATS, VEGETABLES, FRUITS

- Grass-fed ruminants (beef, lamb, and bison) and pastured pork and poultry are ideal.

- Berries are preferred over other fruits.

- Nuts, alcohol, and chocolate are okay if consumed in moderation and treated as pleasure foods.

GREAT: FISH, SEAFOOD, FERMENTED (PROBIOTIC) FOODS, ORGAN MEATS, BROTHS, SEAWEED, EGG YOLKS

- Wild, sustainably-caught seafood is ideal, with the exception of molluscs, which are more sustainable when farmed (see page 248). Consult the Seafood Watch Program run by the Monterey Bay Aquarium.

BAD: CEREAL GRAINS, LEGUMES, DAIRY, PROCESSED FOODS, SUGARS, ADDITIVES

- Cereal grains (wheat, barley, rye, corn, and so on) are becoming increasingly problematic for our digestive systems due to the weakened composition of our gut flora.

- Rice is the only grain I feel is completely okay to eat, as it is extremely low in toxins, especially white rice (see page 26).

- Oils derived from seeds and grains (vegetable, corn, soybean, canola, and the like) are highly inflammatory and likely contribute to the rising rates of cardio-vascular disease and stroke throughout the world.

- Fermented legumes (tamari, miso, natto, and tempeh) are acceptable, as most toxins are destroyed in the fermentation process. Soy is extremely disruptive to the endocrine system and should be avoided as much as possible. Beans that are prepared traditionally (soaked overnight) are superior to canned beans, but they may still cause issues for some people. Green beans, snow peas, sugar snap peas, and even green peas are low in toxins, and I consider them acceptable to eat in moderation.

- Some forms of dairy are better than others, and dairy tolerance is highly individualized (see page 28).

- Certain natural sweeteners, like honey, maple syrup, and coconut palm sugar, are fine in moderation.

To sum it up, I think maintaining health is easy and fun: Eat a variety of good foods. Spend time outdoors. Get a lot of sleep. Minimize stress and addictive behaviors.

For further information about the science behind my dietary and culinary principles, I suggest consulting the following resources:

The Perfect Health Diet: Regain Health and Lose Weight by Eating the Way You Were Meant to Eat, by Paul Jaminet, Ph.D. and Shou-Ching Jaminet, Ph.D.

The Paleo Solution: The Original Human Diet, by Robb Wolf

Your Personal Paleo Code: The 3-Step Plan to Lose Weight, Reverse Disease, and Stay Fit and Healthy for Life, by Chris Kresser

e, Potatoes, and Dairy

se of rice, potatoes, and dairy may appear heretical in a cookbook tailored
leo lifestyle, so I want to clear the air about their presence here. My belief
the Paleo diet has evolved from its first descriptions, as it should, and ap-
ate forms and portions of rice, potatoes, and dairy are excellent additions
dinner table in the amounts that are ideal for you. I do not consider these
to be "cheat" foods, as if they were in violation of a healthy diet.

g followed ancestral eating principles for several years now, I have seen
on patterns in people who eat a strict Paleo diet. For many people, the im-
ntation of strict Paleo over extended periods often results in eating "cheat
' (which they would otherwise avoid on principle) because of powerful
gs, followed by a period of remorse or a compromise in health and weight-
als. I don't think this pattern is healthy. Instead, I think it's important for
to find a diet that works for them, one that doesn't involve moments of
ess or seesaw eating patterns. Food should be a celebration, something to
od about—not a reason to feel guilty. If you cannot sustain a strict Paleo
r more than a few weeks before falling off the wagon, I believe there's
ing wrong with the diet, not you. An optimal diet should be both nour-
and sustainable.

filled with delicious, nutrient-dense foods that are low in toxins and taken
diversity of sources is ideal. This is the same principle underlying a strict
diet. But one overlooked fact is that the key to health is getting *enough*
nutrients. You can still get enough nutrients while eating some foods that are
nutritionally poor compared to others, including rice and potatoes. Few people
would argue that iceberg lettuce and celery are evil foods, but they're also nutritionally poor. That doesn't mean you can't eat them. Likewise, adding dairy
to dishes makes them more satisfying and adds a significant depth of flavor. It is
this variety that creates health, keeps meals interesting, and gives you the tools
and power to sustain a lifetime of healthy eating choices.

If you're worried about the carbohydrate content of rice, potatoes, and starch-
based flours, whether you choose to eat them will be dependent on your weight-
loss goals. All the same, the carbohydrate content of these foods is definitely
manageable. A diet containing less than 150 grams of carbs a day is often considered low-carb and contributes to a steady loss of body fat: 1 pound of cooked
rice contains 125 grams of carbs, 1 pound of white potatoes contains 87 grams of
carbs, and 1 pound of sweet potatoes contains 80 grams of carbs. So while white
rice and potatoes are more carb-intensive than other foods, you can still enjoy
them and maintain a low-carb lifestyle.

I fully acknowledge that these foods may be problematic for some people, especially those who suffer from an autoimmune or allergy issue. See pages 275-278
for my chart on how to adjust this book's recipes for a stricter version of Paleo.

Rice

Rice figures prominently in this book, but many people argue that white rice has no place in the Paleo diet because it is a grain. What first led me down the path of questioning the idea that rice isn't "Paleo" is that it doesn't make sense from a historical perspective. Historians estimate that the progenitor of rice existed some 130 million years ago—well before humans came on the scene.[1] Wild rice was eaten by prehistoric peoples, and it was first domesticated around 13,000 years ago, well before the end of the Paleolithic era and a couple thousand years before wheat was domesticated. Second, rice has a reputation among many traditional cultures as being a safe food for digestion; indeed, congee (see page 106 for my recipe) is a common food served worldwide to people who are ill and need to digest calories without upsetting their stomachs.

Rice has by far the lowest toxicity of all the cereal grains, and most of its toxins exist in the rice bran, which is the covering around the kernel (found in brown rice). Therefore, I recommend eating only white rice. There are concerns that rice contains phytic acid, which is a known toxin, but it may surprise you to learn that rice has less phytic acid than many foods approved by common Paleo diet standards, such as coconut, avocados, walnuts, almonds, coriander seeds, and sesame seeds.[2] Additionally, the vast majority of the toxins that remain in white rice are destroyed in the cooking process.

Rice isn't exactly nutritious when compared to meats, fruits, and vegetables, so I like to increase its nutritional profile by cooking it in broth (as in my recipes for Seafood Paella, page 241; and Mexican Rice, page 103) or with other foods like coconut milk, butter, ghee, and turmeric (Basic Steamed Rice, page 96). When my family does eat rice plain, we top it with furikake, a Japanese rice seasoning made from seaweed, dried fish, and sesame seeds. All of these additions make rice both delicious and more nutritious.

Consider this: a meal of chicken breasts, lettuce, and steamed broccoli is technically "Paleo," while a recipe like my Dirty Rice (page 100) is often not considered "Paleo" at all. But look at the ingredients used to make dirty rice: butter, vegetables, broth, chicken livers, gizzards, and sausage. I would argue that dirty rice has a much more robust nutritional profile than the "Paleo" meal above, despite the fact that it's made with 1½ cups of white rice spread out among six guests. And I'll let you guess as to which dish is more delicious and rewarding and less prone to make you want to jump off the deep end to satisfy food cravings.

Rice isn't eaten on its own, either, but as part of a whole meal, often with fats and acids; evidence suggests that eating carbs combined with fats and acids improves their digestibility and reduces blood sugar spikes.[3] This combination naturally occurs in most traditional meals, including those found in this book. Also bear in mind that rices differ in glycemic load. Basmati rice is a long-grain rice that has a very low glycemic load and can be used in place of short-grain or medium-grain white rice in this book. Jasmine rice is long-grain but carries a very high glycemic load, and is not used in this book.

Potatoes

Potatoes are also a source of controversy in the Paleo and ancestral communities, despite the widespread acknowledgement that underground storage organs, otherwise known as tubers, are an important staple food for nearly every indigenous culture on the planet. They were likely important during the Paleolithic era as well.[4]

Potatoes have a fair amount of nutrients, including potassium, magnesium, and vitamin C. They are also relatively free of toxins. Glycoalkaloids, their most prominent toxin, are significantly reduced when the potatoes are peeled and cooked gently (most traditional cultures peeled their potatoes). Modern potatoes were also cultivated over time to reduce glycoalkaloids and improve digestibility; russet potatoes have some of the lowest levels of toxins in potatoes today. There are studies showing that potatoes increase inflammation markers in some people, and the potato's status as a pro-inflammatory nightshade is due to its glycoalkaloid content. This effect may be more attributable to the form (fried potato chips) or skin content of the potatoes used in these studies. In other words, eating peeled and boiled potatoes is less inflammatory than eating fried potatoes or potato skins.

Some forms of potatoes encourage overeating, which gives potatoes in general a bad reputation. Scientists have developed what they call the Satiety Index, which rates foods by how good they are at satisfying hunger. Boiled potatoes were the most satiating food, far outpacing and nearly doubling the next foods on the list, fish and beef. Potato chips and French fries, however, were only one-third as satisfying as boiled potatoes, which means that you could eat three times as many potatoes in the form of French fries or chips before feeling full.[5] This is why you can eat a whole basket of fries or an entire bag of chips and not feel satisfied, but can barely make it through one or two boiled potatoes.

Sweet potatoes were on the original list of "approved" Paleo foods when the diet was first emerging, because white potatoes had a higher toxin profile and contained fewer nutrients. Sweet potatoes have the same carb content and glycemic load as white potatoes. Today, many Paleo nutritionists concede that when cooked properly, white potatoes can have a place on the dinner table equal to sweet potatoes.

Every form of potato in this book is peeled in order to minimize the glycoalkaloid content and gently cooked by baking or boiling.

Dairy

Let's talk about why dairy is in this book in the first place. Dairy is an excellent source of calcium, and it is hard to get an adequate amount of calcium just from eating greens and certain fish unless you're prepared to eat fish heads often. Dairy is also a good source of vitamins A, D, and K2, nutrients that are sometimes difficult to find in other foods. While conventional wisdom associates high-fat dairy with obesity, cardiovascular disease, and metabolic disease, observational studies have found the opposite to be true.[6]

From a culinary perspective, dairy products are essential in any refined kitchen. Butter imparts delicious flavor when cooked at medium and low heats. Cream adds body and depth of flavor, and cheese is overwhelmingly delicious. So I believe that there are nutritional and culinary reasons to find out how to prudently incorporate dairy into our diets.

The major reason people have issues with digesting dairy is that they lack the enzyme called lactase, which is highly dependent on ancestry; only about 40% of us maintain the enzyme past childhood. It's also highly dependent on the state of bacteria growth in an individual's digestive system.

Even if you've had issues with dairy in the past, you may still be able to enjoy dairy again. As popular Paleo health practitioner Chris Kresser points out in his excellent blog (www.chriskresser.com), symptoms related to lactose intolerance can often be alleviated through the use of probiotic supplements and small doses of yogurt (a few spoonfuls a day).[7] His process is a long-term solution for those hoping to heal their gut issues so that they may be able to eat dairy again one day. For ten years I believed that I had a form of lactose intolerance and avoided dairy. But after a couple years of eating my version of Paleo, which includes daily probiotic foods, I found that I had little to no issues eating most forms of dairy. For more information, check out Chris's article in the references that follow.

Not all forms of dairy are equal. First and foremost, if you are ever in a position to consume raw dairy (which highly depends on the state you live in), DO IT. Many people who have adverse reactions to pasteurized dairy don't have issues with raw dairy. If you don't have access to raw dairy, try to find pasteurized dairy from grass-fed cows; grass-fed dairy products have a significant amount of vitamin K2. Fermented dairy products like yogurt, kefir, sour cream, and hard cheeses are often better tolerated than milk. Butter and cream also have less lactose in them since they have a higher fat content than milk. Ghee, a form of clarified butter, has its milk solids separated from the fat and is generally easier to digest than butter. All the same, you'll find that the dairy amounts in most of my recipes are negligible or easily substituted (see pages 275-278 for my substitution guide). Experimenting with the milk of other mammals (for example, goat's or sheep's milk) for cheese and yogurt is another option.

To summarize, dairy fats are excellent sources of calories, but lactose can be problematic; however, lactose intolerance is often affected by overall gut health. Improving your gut health by eating probiotic foods (many are found in the Vegetables chapter of this book) may improve your ability to digest dairy. My advice is to find out what works for you and to challenge it every once in a while. Healing your gut bacteria can take a long time, so I would try dairy every few months to see how your body reacts to it.

References

[1]"Rice." *The Cambridge World History of Food*. Ed. Kenneth F. Kiple and Kriemhild Coneè Ornelas. www.cambridge.org/us/books/kiple/rice.htm

[2]"Phytic Acid in Common 'Paleo' Foods." HuntGatherLove. Melissa McEwen. huntgatherlove. com/content/phytic-acid-common-paleo-foods

[3]"Glycemic Index of Single and Mixed Meal Foods among Common Japanese Foods with White Rice as a Reference Food." *European Journal of Clinical Nutrition*. M. Sugiyama, A. C. Tang, Y. Wakaki, and W. Yokama. www.ncbi.nlm.nih.gov/pubmed/12792658

[4]"A Multidisciplinary Deconstruction of Palaeolithic Nutrition That Holds Promise for the Prevention and Treatment of Diseases of Civilisation." *Nutrition Research Reviews*. Remko S. Kuipers, Josephine C. A. Joordens, and Frits A. J. Muskiet. dx.doi.org/10.1017/S0954422412000017

[5]"A Satiety Index of Common Foods." *European Journal of Clinical Nutrition*. S. H. Holt, J. C. Miller, P. Petocz, and E. Farmakalidis. www.ncbi.nlm.nih.gov/pubmed/7498104 (chart: www. mendosa.com/satiety.htm)

[6]"The Relationship Between High-Fat Dairy Consumption and Obesity, Cardiovascular, and Metabolic Disease." *European Journal of Nutrition*. M. Kratz, T. Baars, and S. Guyenet. www.ncbi. nlm.nih.gov/pubmed/22810464

[7]"How to Cure Lactose Intolerance." Chris Kresser. www.chriskresser.com/how-to-cure-lactose-intolerance

Less-Common Pantry Ingredients

RICE WINES

The recipes in this book use three types of rice wine: mirin, a sweet rice wine; saké, a Japanese rice wine; and Chinese cooking wine, which is sometimes called Chinese sherry or Shaoxing wine. Look for high-quality wines that are free of corn syrup; since they are generally used sparingly, they will last a long time.

WHEAT-FREE TAMARI

Tamari is the original soy sauce introduced to Japan from China, and it is made without wheat. While most forms of soy are best avoided, I think that fermented forms of soy (tamari, miso, natto, and tempeh) are okay; of those four, only tamari is represented in this book. Tamari is the liquid that is left over when making miso. It has a much bolder and sharper taste than many other soy sauces, so I often cut its sharp taste with honey, as you'll see in the recipes.

FISH SAUCE

Much like anchovy paste, fish sauce is an easy way to add umami flavors and is used in many Asian dishes. Fish sauce is usually made from fermented anchovies. Don't let the initial fishiness of the sauce fool you—adding it to a dish often creates a very un-fish-like flavor. Look for varieties without added sugar, like Red Boat Fish Sauce.

SHRIMP PASTE

Shrimp paste, made from fermented shrimp, is a common flavor enhancer in Southeast Asia. It is similar to fish sauce but often more pungent. I prefer the terasi version, which is sold in blocks, but it is sometimes hard to find. Shrimp sauce, a Chinese invention, is a saltier version of shrimp paste and is more easily found. Adjust salt levels in your recipes accordingly.

CHINESE GREENS

There are four major kinds of Chinese greens found in this book:

Bok choy – Both bulbous and leafy, bok choy is the most popular of the Chinese greens. It can have a white or green stem. Immature cabbages are often sold as baby bok choy.

Choy sum – A slender version of bok choy with thick, cylindrical stems; it is sometimes called flowering Chinese cabbage (pictured in my Chinese Greens recipe, page 82).

Kai-lan – Also known as Chinese broccoli, kai-lan also has thick stems. It looks like choy sum, has a flavor similar to broccoli, and has small, edible flower heads (pictured in my Chicken Pad See Ew recipe, page 200).

Won bok – Also known as Chinese or napa cabbage, won bok is a large, dense cabbage not unlike head cabbage. It is most commonly used in Kimchi (page 72) or sliced and added to Nabemono (page 256) or Fried Rice (page 104).

FLOURS AND STARCHES

I use a wide variety of flours and starches to replace wheat flour and corn-starch. Rice flour (not to be confused with sweet rice flour, also known as mochiko) is my go-to flour for thickening; coconut flour can also be used, but it has a grittier texture. Almond flour and coarse-ground almond meal work well in small amounts, especially as a binder. Arrowroot and potato starches are suitable replacements for cornstarch. Tapioca starch acts as a starch but can become stretchy; this property is desirable in some contexts, like in my pizza crust recipe (page 122).

SWEETENERS

My favorite sweeteners are pure honey and maple syrup, but others should be noted. Coconut palm sugar is made from the sap of coconut palm flower buds and is often sold in granulated form. It is the closest substitute for real sugar out there, and it is used sparingly in some dishes in this book. Palm sugar, often confused with coconut palm sugar, is made from the sap of the Arenga pinnata (sugar palm) and is used to sweeten Southeast Asian dishes.

SPICES

It is worth your time to invest in a robust spice rack; having and knowing a wide variety of spices will greatly expand your breadth of cooking. Some less-common spices found in this book include cardamom pods, dried fenugreek leaves (kasuri methi) and seeds, Kashmiri red chili powder, mace, Korean red chili powder (gochugaru), turmeric, and white pepper.

SALTS

Sea salt is harvested from evaporated seawater and contains trace minerals; I used fine sea salt in developing these recipes, which has an equal saltiness and texture to table salt. I also used Morton's kosher salt when writing this book; if you use the other leading brand, Diamond Crystal, you'll need about one-third more salt, because it is significantly less salty than Morton's.

Bok Choy

Choy Sum

Won Bok

Tools

DUTCH OR FRENCH OVEN

Easily the most-used pot in my kitchen, a 5-quart Dutch (or French) oven is worth its weight in gold. It can be used to brown, braise, and simmer dishes with an even heat distribution, and it works like a charm in the oven.

STAINLESS-STEEL SKILLET

I often use a 10" to 14" stainless-steel skillet when I don't need the tall sides of a Dutch oven. Stainless-steel skillets work especially well for oven-roasting meats because you can make a gravy directly in the pan with the drippings that accumulate.

CAST-IRON SKILLET

Another essential, a 10" to 12" cast-iron skillet is superior for frying and roasting at high temperatures.

LARGE STOCKPOT

Perfect for boiling, simmering, and steaming. With the amount of broths my family makes, our 8-quart stockpot always seems to be on the stove.

RIMMED BAKING SHEET WITH WIRE RACK

Called a half sheet in the culinary world, this versatile 13" x 8" sheet can be used to roast any number of dishes, and an accompanying 12" x 7" rack enables you to keep ingredients dry.

BLENDER OR FOOD PROCESSOR

A blender or food processor is necessary to create appealing sauces and mixes and can save you time in the kitchen so you can be outdoors with your family instead. In addition to a stand-alone blender or food processor, an immersion blender is an inexpensive but useful tool for blending soups and sauces in large amounts without having to transfer them to another container.

STRAINER AND CHEESECLOTH

Paired with a blender, a strainer (with or without cheesecloth) can create velvety sauces and clear broths and will make your dishes much more appealing to the eye.

SHARP KNIFE

A sharp knife seriously lessens the drudgery of cutting. I prefer a 10" Santoku or chef's knife. Be sure to get an appropriate sharpener to keep your knife in good condition.

QUICK-READ THERMOMETER

Essential for knowing when meats and oils reach the desired temperature.

CHIMNEY STARTER

Worth its weight in gold if you use a charcoal grill, a chimney starter quickly and effortlessly lights and warms charcoal without lighter fluid.

Cooking Techniques

BLANCH

To submerge a food in boiling water for a short time (often 30 seconds or less) to cook it slightly but retain its shape, color, and/or texture. Also referred to as parboiling.

BLEND

To grind into a smooth paste or liquid using a blender or food processor on a high setting. Blending produces smoother results than processing.

BRAISE

To simmer, generally covered, in a liquid over low heat.

COMBINE

To mix ingredients together, generally gently so as to not disturb the foods. When applicable, I combine ingredients with my hands.

CHOP, DICE, AND MINCE

Chopping is the most coarse cutting technique, resulting in large, uneven chunks. Dicing produces small, even pieces about ¼" in size. Mincing involves chopping an ingredient as finely as possible. Think of it this way: in a salad you could use chopped lettuce, diced eggs and tomatoes, and minced ham.

DEGLAZE

To add liquid (usually broth or wine) to a pan that has browned chunks stuck to it and simmer the liquid while scraping up and whisking the chunks (called sucs) into the liquid to form a flavorful sauce.

FOLD

To combine a light ingredient with a heavier ingredient while retaining as much air as possible. To fold, add the light ingredient to the heavier one and cut through the mixture with the edge of a spatula, moving in a figure-eight motion and rotating the bowl as you go. When the spatula gets to the side of the bowl, scrape the side to incorporate the lighter ingredient into the mixture. This technique is hard to describe with words—your best bet is to watch a couple online videos of this technique in action.

JULIENNE

To cut ingredients into long, thin, matchstick-shaped sticks.

PROCESS

To grind into a somewhat chunky paste or liquid using a blender or food processor on a lower or pulse setting.

REDUCE

To simmer a liquid on medium or higher heat to evaporate some of the water content and deepen the flavor.

SAUTÉ	To cook dry ingredients on medium or high heat with some oil or fat to keep the ingredients from sticking to the pan.
SIMMER	To heat a liquid on medium or low heat so that it bubbles but does not boil.
SWEAT	To gently sauté vegetables (usually onions or other aromatics) on lower heat to evaporate the liquid and lessen any sharp or astringent flavors.

Grilling and Smoking Basics

CHARCOAL FUEL AND GRILLING TEMPERATURES

Charcoal grills use two main types of fuel: hardwood charcoal and briquettes. Hardwood charcoal creates a hot and fast-burning fire; briquettes are generally cooler and last longer. To put it more simply, hardwood makes for great steaks, and briquettes are good for barbecue. The easiest way to start a charcoal fire is to employ a chimney starter, which usually uses a little newspaper to start the fire in lieu of lighter fluid.

The thermometers found on the lids of grills are generally inaccurate. Buying a remote grill thermometer can take the guesswork out of grilling. If you don't have a grill thermometer, an easy way to gauge grill temperature is to see how long you can comfortably hold your hand above the fire, about 5" from the cooking grates: hot = 2 seconds, medium-hot = 3 to 4 seconds, medium = 5 to 6 seconds, and medium-low = 7 seconds.

DIRECT GRILLING

Direct grilling is cooking foods directly over the heat, creating a delicious crust caused by the Maillard reaction (also known as the browning reaction). Direct grilling is the easiest cooking method but can burn the outside of the food before it is done on the inside. It is best combined with indirect grilling for foods that require extended cooking times.

INDIRECT GRILLING

Indirect grilling occurs when you limit the heat to one side of the grill and keep the other side cool, placing your food on the cool side of the grill. With a charcoal grill, this is done by banking the coals on one side, often with a large aluminum pan under the cool side of the grill to catch drippings and prevent the coals from sliding under the meat. With a gas grill, it's done by turning off some of the burners; you'll need to experiment with your gas grill to find how many burners to turn off in order to get the temperatures you want. Indirect grilling enables you to cook foods on the grill without burning them or causing flare-ups from dripping fat. It is often combined with short amounts of direct grilling to create a delicious crust and a fully cooked inside.

INDIRECT SMOKING

Indirect smoking is similar to indirect grilling, but with wood chunks and wood chips placed over the fire. With a gas grill, fill two smoker boxes or small aluminum pans with wood chips and wood chunks, as shown in the illustration on page 35. Add about ½" water to the wood chips. Place the smoker boxes on the side of the grill that will be hot and a large aluminum pan on the side of the grill that will be cool. As the wood chunks burn and smoke, the water in the wood chips will evaporate and eventually burn and smoke, but usually after the wood chunks have burnt out. This will enable you to smoke meats for an extended period without having to add wood. When smoking with a charcoal grill, you can add wood chunks directly to the charcoal, adding more as they burn out. Bear in mind that meats do not need to be smoked the entire time; an hour or two in a smoky environment is generally sufficient.

Hickory is an excellent all-purpose smoking wood that works well with both pork and beef. Fruit woods like apple and cherry are milder, sweeter, and ideal for both pork and poultry.

CHAPTER 2

SAUCES, CONDIMENTS, AND OTHER BASICS

Rendered Fat Basics

One of the most challenging parts of starting a new, healthy lifestyle is understanding the importance of using the right fats in cooking. In addition to coconut oil, olive oil, and butter, rendered fats from healthy animals are excellent energy sources. Here is a quick guide on how to render your own animal fats.

LARD

One of the most versatile animal-based cooking fats, lard is rendered pig fat. It is stable at high heat and is the superior choice for frying. Lard can be made from back or leaf fat (the area around the pig's kidneys); leaf fat has a more neutral taste.

To make lard, cut the fat into the smallest pieces possible, trimming away any skin or meat. Partially freezing the fat beforehand makes it easier to cut. A meat grinder is the easiest and most effective way to cut the lard to an appropriate size.

Cook the fat in a skillet or Dutch oven on low, pouring and straining the liquid fat through a coffee filter or cheesecloth as it accumulates. Once the pieces turn golden brown and stop rendering lard, the fat has been fully rendered; strain the remaining liquid fat and reserve the browned fat pieces, known as lardons, to add to soups, salads, or Guacamole (page 56) as a flavor enhancer. This process can take up to 2 hours total. Be extra careful not to heat lard on anything higher than low, as the fat burns easily and burnt lard is inedible.

Alternatively, you can render the lard in water to guarantee that it won't burn, a process called wet rendering. This method yields less lard than dry rendering but is worry-free. Add the minced fat to a stockpot with a few cups of water; bring to a boil, reduce the heat, and simmer on low for at least 2 hours and up to 4 hours. Strain the fat pieces and separate the rendered lard from the water using a fat separator. The fat pieces can later be crisped in a skillet to make lardons, if desired.

TALLOW

Tallow is rendered beef, bison, or lamb fat. To cook it, use the same process described above for lard. Tallow is also an excellent high-heat fat and has a similarly high smoke point, but it tends to have a meatier taste than lard.

DUCK FAT

Eating potatoes or vegetables roasted in duck fat is an unforgettable experience. Rendering duck fat is possible, but finding skin and fat on their own is difficult. I prefer to create and reserve duck fat when roasting a whole duck (page 211) or to buy rendered fat from a high-quality supplier like Fatworks.

SCHMALTZ

Schmaltz is rendered chicken or goose fat. It is used primarily as a spread and a frying fat in Eastern Europe and in many Jewish communities. It is also commonly used to make chicken liver pâté. Schmaltz can be used to make a roux, which occurs naturally when making my Roasted Chicken (page 190).

GHEE

Ghee is a form of clarified butter and is an excellent cooking fat. It differs from regular clarified butter in that the milk solids are left to brown in the butter as it simmers, adding a nutty flavor. Because its milk solids, which tend to burn at high temperatures, are rendered out, ghee can be used to cook foods at high heat while still imparting a rich, buttery taste. To clarify butter, heat it on low, gently simmering until the milk solids bubble, separate, and turn golden brown, 10 to 15 minutes. Strain through at least two layers of cheesecloth, let cool, and store in the fridge for up to several months. Two cups butter yields 1½ cups ghee.

Stock and Broth Basics

Stocks and broths are essential elements of many savory dishes. They are nutrient-dense and renowned as healing foods throughout the world (think chicken soup). Perhaps just as important is the fact that they enhance flavors. The term stock *generally refers to a liquid made by simmering bones, meat, and vegetables;* broth *refers to a stock that has been seasoned with salt, pepper, tomato paste, and/or wine. In the United States, the word* stock *can imply that it was simmered with only bones and vegetables. Most home chefs use the two terms interchangeably. I tend to season my stock into broth so that I can enjoy a plain cup of broth when I feel like it. In general, I prefer to use a combination of two-thirds bones to one-third meats, or bones with generous portions of meat attached.*

BEEF, BISON, VEAL, AND LAMB STOCK/BROTH

2-3 LBS. SOUP BONES COMBINED WITH MEATY BONES (OXTAILS, SHANKS, KNUCKLE BONES, ETC.)

1 LARGE ONION, SKIN INTACT, QUARTERED

3-4 LARGE CARROTS, TOPS INTACT, CUT IN HALF LENGTHWISE

3-4 STALKS CELERY, WITH LEAVES, CUT IN HALF LENGTHWISE

1 TBSP. BLACK PEPPERCORNS

6 CLOVES GARLIC

3 SPRIGS FRESH DILL

3 SPRIGS FRESH PARSLEY

2 TBSP. TOMATO PASTE

SALT AND BLACK PEPPER TO TASTE

1. Place the bones on a rimmed baking sheet, then place in the oven and broil until well browned, about 20 minutes. Add to a large stockpot, fill the pot with enough cold water to cover the bones by 1", then boil on high heat for 10 minutes. Drain and rinse the bones in cold water, then clean the pot; return the bones to the pot and add the remaining ingredients. Fill with enough water to cover everything by 1". Bring to a boil, cover, and reduce the heat to low; simmer for at least 2 hours or up to 12 hours, adding water as it evaporates. Alternatively, you can simmer the bones in a slow cooker.

2. Strain and discard the solids, and add salt and pepper to taste. Pour the broth into a fat separator, then distribute into jars. Allow to cool, then refrigerate for up to 2 weeks or freeze for up to 6 months.

For Pork (or Ham) Stock/Broth: Use pigs' feet, hocks, or neck bones. Pork is naturally saltier than beef, so be sure to taste it before seasoning. Leftover ham bones are excellent sources of stock and do not require roasting ahead of time.

For Poultry Stock/Broth: Use feet, necks, and backs, which don't need to be roasted ahead of time. Substitute ½ cup white wine for the tomato paste. Carcasses from whole roasted chickens, ducks, or turkeys can also be used to make stock.

FISH STOCK/BROTH

1 TBSP. BUTTER

1 LARGE CARROT, COARSELY CHOPPED

1 LARGE ONION, COARSELY CHOPPED

1 STALK CELERY, COARSELY CHOPPED

10 BLACK PEPPERCORNS

1 CUP WHITE WINE

1-2 LBS. FISH HEADS, BONES, AND TAILS, GILLS AND INTESTINES REMOVED (WHITE, NON-OILY FISH SUCH AS HALIBUT, COD, SOLE, ROCKFISH, OR SNAPPER PREFERRED)

5 SPRIGS FRESH PARSLEY

2 BAY LEAVES

1. Melt the butter in a large stockpot on medium heat. Add the carrot, onion, celery, and peppercorns and sauté until softened, 5 minutes. Add the white wine and bring to a simmer, then add the remaining ingredients and 2-3 quarts water. Once simmering, reduce the heat to low and gently simmer for 2 hours without stirring. Skim off any foam that accumulates.

2. Strain into jars using a colander and 2 layers of cheesecloth, discarding the solids. Keep in the fridge for up to a week or in the freezer for up to a month.

For Shellfish Stock/Broth: Use crab, lobster, shrimp, and crawfish shells. Shrimp and crawfish heads can also be included.

Gravy Basics

Mastering gravies and pan sauces is an essential way to enhance a dish's flavor and provide moisture. They are also an excellent way to make sure that pan drippings and braising liquids don't go to waste. The term pan sauce *is generally reserved for sauces made by deglazing a pan after browning or pan-frying that are usually thin in texture. In the United States, however,* gravy *is a general term that can include thickened sauces made from braising liquid or broth, as well as pan sauces.*

ROUX-BASED GRAVY

A roux is a mixture of flour and fat used to thicken gravies and soups. A roux made of wheat flour is extremely forgiving; many chefs make the roux separately and stir it into the liquid to thicken it. Rice and coconut flours are less forgiving and unpredictable, so it is better to make your grain-free roux in a large skillet and then add liquid to the skillet until it reaches the desired thickness. A roux made with white rice flour and butter is most consistently like a wheat-based roux in terms of flavor and texture and is my preferred roux. If you roast your meat in a stainless-steel skillet (like Roasted Chicken, page 190), you can create your roux directly in the skillet, drippings included.

1-2 TBSP. COOKING FAT (BUTTER, RESERVED BACON DRIPPINGS, LARD, OR COCONUT OIL)

1-2 TBSP. WHITE RICE FLOUR OR COCONUT FLOUR

1-2 CUPS DRIPPINGS, BROTH, WINE, BRAISING LIQUID, OR A COMBINATION

SALT AND BLACK PEPPER TO TASTE

1. Heat the fat in a large skillet on medium-low until warmed, about 1 minute. Add the flour and stir to combine, then toast the roux until golden brown, about 3 minutes. Stir in the drippings, broth, wine, or braising liquid and bring to a simmer, adding more liquid as it thickens. Some gravies fare better with some cream added, as in Chicken-Fried Steak (page 134). If you have leftover scraps from carving the meat, mince the scraps and add them to the gravy. Season with salt and pepper to taste and serve.

2. Gravy broths can be premade (page 42) or, when cooking whole poultry, created by simmering the giblets (neck and gizzard, not the liver) as it roasts. Adding a splash of white wine to chicken broth or red wine to beef broth adds depth of flavor; the acidity also helps with the digestion of starches, like Garlic Mashed Potatoes (page 108) or Rice (page 96).

PAN SAUCES

Pan sauces, like that in my Eye of Round Roast recipe (page 129), are even simpler because they reach the desired taste and consistency through reduction. Typically, braising liquid, broth, or wine is combined with the browned bits left over from browning (called sucs, from the French) and reduced and seasoned. Pan sauces are often strained before serving for presentation's sake.

SUCS (BROWNED PIECES FROM BROWNING)

1-2 CUPS BRAISING LIQUID, BROTH, WINE, OR A COMBINATION

SALT AND BLACK PEPPER TO TASTE

1. Pour the braising liquid, broth, and wine into the pan used to brown the meat, whisking the liquid together with the sucs to deglaze the pan. Simmer on medium heat until reduced to your desired consistency (reducing by half is typical), then season with salt and pepper to taste and serve.

Gravies can also be thickened by using a starch-based slurry. As a general rule, 1 Tbsp. starch will easily thicken 1 cup liquid. For anything beyond 2 cups liquid, I prefer to use arrowroot starch, as potato starch can clump in larger quantities. Arrowroot starch maintains its thickness when it cools; potato starch does not.

I do not recommend using tapioca starch as a thickener, as it creates a gummy texture. Some people like to use small amounts of gelatin to thicken gravies, but I find that it's too easy to overthicken the gravy into something more akin to Jell-O.

STARCH-THICKENED GRAVY

1-2 CUPS DRIPPINGS, BROTH, WINE, BRAISING LIQUID, OR A COMBINATION

SALT AND BLACK PEPPER TO TASTE

1-2 TBSP. POTATO STARCH OR ARROWROOT STARCH

1-2 TBSP. COLD WATER

1. Combine the drippings, broth, and wine, season to taste with salt and pepper, and bring to a simmer over medium heat. Whisk together the starch and cold water into a slurry in a small bowl; add the slurry to the gravy and stir until thickened.

Barbecue Rubs

When I was first adopting a whole-foods diet, I had a hard time finding barbecue rubs that were both affordable and free of additives. While beef fares very well without any added sweetener in the rub, both poultry and pork develop a much more intense and exciting flavor when paired with some coconut palm sugar.

Chipotle chili powder is my preferred powder for barbecue rubs, but feel free to change it to suit your tastes: ancho (less spicy and sweeter), guajillo (less spicy but smoky), cayenne (spicier), and jalapeño (even spicier) powders all work well.

ALL-PURPOSE BEEF RUB

YIELDS: 1 CUP

4 TBSP. KOSHER SALT

4 TBSP. PAPRIKA

2 TBSP. BLACK PEPPER

2 TBSP. GARLIC POWDER

2 TSP. ONION POWDER

1 TSP. GROUND CELERY SEED

1 TSP. DRIED OREGANO

1 TSP. CHIPOTLE CHILI POWDER

ALL-PURPOSE PORK AND POULTRY RUB

YIELDS: 1 CUP

4 TBSP. BLACK PEPPER

4 TBSP. COCONUT PALM SUGAR

4 TBSP. PAPRIKA

3 TBSP. KOSHER SALT

2 TSP. CHIPOTLE CHILI POWDER

2 TSP. GARLIC POWDER

2 TSP. ONION POWDER

1. To make the rubs, simply combine the ingredients and store in airtight containers. These rubs work well with all smoked meats and can be used with dishes that use direct grilling as well. Experimenting with different chili powders will add a surprising amount of variety.

Barbecue Sauce

The exact origin of barbecue sauce is unclear, but it started appearing in written documents as early as the 1600s as a product of the New World. This makes sense considering that both tomatoes and peppers came from the Americas and are key components of this flavorful sauce.

There are countless variations of barbecue sauce. Some of the most prominent regional favorites are from Kansas City (sweet), South Carolina (mustard-based), Texas (not sweet, often mixed with beef drippings as in my Barbecue Brisket recipe, page 138), and Tennessee (mixed with whiskey). The most common commercial barbecue sauces are Kansas City sauces. Memphis barbecue is unique in that a dry rub is preferred over a sauce, with the sauce often served on the side; Memphis sauces are similar to Kansas City sauces but with more vinegar. My recipe is modeled after Memphis-style sauces: sweet, tangy, with just a hint of spiciness.

It's amazing how much time (and how many ingredients) it takes to make a good barbecue sauce. If you're planning on making your own, be sure to set aside several hours to get the flavors right. The act of making barbecue sauce itself is pretty easy—cook some onions, add the rest of the ingredients, simmer, and blend. The trick is balancing the hefty ingredients list to get the taste you want.

YIELDS: 6 CUPS

PREP TIME: 5 MINUTES

COOKING TIME: 3 HOURS

2 TBSP. COCONUT OIL

2 MEDIUM ONIONS, MINCED

2 (28 OZ.) CANS WHOLE TOMATOES IN JUICE

2 (8 OZ.) CANS TOMATO SAUCE

1 1/2 CUPS APPLE CIDER VINEGAR

1/2 CUP HONEY

4 TBSP. MOLASSES (BLACKSTRAP OR DATE MOLASSES)

1/2 CUP ORANGE JUICE

1/4 CUP DIJON MUSTARD

2 TBSP. PAPRIKA

2 TBSP. CHILI POWDER

1 TBSP. BLACK PEPPER

1 TBSP. HICKORY LIQUID SMOKE

2 TSP. SEA SALT

2 TSP. WORCESTERSHIRE SAUCE

1/2 TSP. ALLSPICE

2 BAY LEAVES

1. In a stockpot, warm the coconut oil on medium heat for 1 minute, then add the onions and sauté until softened, about 6 minutes. Add the remaining ingredients; bring to a simmer, reduce the heat to low, and simmer, uncovered, for 2 hours, stirring occasionally.

2. Remove the bay leaves and blend the sauce with an immersion blender (or in batches in a blender) until smooth. Simmer for another 30 minutes. Season with salt and pepper to taste, and add more honey or molasses to thicken if needed.

3. The sauce will keep in the refrigerator for a month but can be preserved by canning for up to a year. To can the sauce, sterilize 3 pint-sized canning jars by boiling them in a stockpot lined with a steamer rack, with at least 1" water above the jars, for 10 minutes. Remove the jars and drain, but keep the water boiling; pour the sauce into the jars, cover, then submerge them in the hot water bath for 45 minutes. Remove the jars and leave them out to cool overnight. Verify that the canning worked by checking to see if the lids have sucked down into the jars.

Mayonnaise

While the origin of the word mayonnaise *is the subject of some dispute, it's clear that the beloved white sauce is of French origin, appearing in the 1700s.*

It's difficult to find the right oil to make a good mayonnaise. Avocado and macadamia nut oils are excellent but pricey. High-oleic sunflower oil has a decent health profile and is relatively inexpensive. Coconut oil works but creates a strange mouth feel and sometimes an overly hard mayo. Extra-virgin olive oil results in a bitter mayo, although mixing it with lard can counteract that bitterness. Light olive oil works well, but you have to make sure that it's from a high-quality source. In the end, I prefer to use a mixture of avocado oil and light olive oil for the best combination of taste and affordability.

Note that you can use one whole egg instead of two egg yolks; I prefer a more nutrient-dense mayo, but a whole-egg mayo will be whiter and will thicken (emulsify) more easily.

YIELDS: 1 CUP
PREP TIME: 30 MINUTES
COOKING TIME: 5 MINUTES

2 EGG YOLKS (OR 1 WHOLE EGG)

1/2 TBSP. LEMON JUICE

1/2 TBSP. WHITE WINE VINEGAR
(WHITE VINEGAR IS OKAY)

1/2 TSP. SEA SALT

1/2 TSP. WHITE PEPPER

1 TSP. DIJON MUSTARD

3/4 CUP AVOCADO OR MACADAMIA
NUT OIL

1/4 CUP LIGHT OLIVE OIL

1. Combine the egg yolks, lemon juice, white wine vinegar, salt, pepper, and mustard in a bowl. Let it sit for 30 minutes to come to room temperature.

2. Combine the oils. Vigorously whip the egg mixture with a whisk, then slowly drizzle in the oil in a constant light stream as you continue to whip. Everything will start to thicken almost immediately. Continue drizzling in the oil until everything is well mixed and deliciously thick. Alternatively, you can put the egg mixture in a wide-mouth jar and use an immersion blender while pouring in the oil. If you don't have an immersion blender, you can use a blender or food processor (on a low setting) and slowly drizzle in the oil.

3. Refrigerate the mayonnaise for 1 hour before using. Be sure to check the expiration date of your eggs; that is how long your mayo will keep.

Basic Red Sauce

Although tomatoes arrived in Europe from the New World in the 16th century, tomato-based sauces didn't start appearing on record until the late 18th century. There is a staggering amount of variation to this seemingly simple sauce: In the United States, marinara *means a simple tomato-based sauce, but in Italy it often refers to a seafood sauce. The term* tomato sauce *can refer to any tomato-based sauce, except in the U.K., Australia, New Zealand, and South Africa, where it refers to ketchup (*pasta sauce *is the proper term in those countries). Neapolitan is a meatless tomato sauce linked to southern Italy. A ragù is a tomato sauce with meat (often referred to as Bolognese sauce outside of Italy).*

YIELDS: 1 QUART
PREP TIME: 10 MINUTES
COOKING TIME: 2 1/2 HOURS

1 TBSP. OLIVE OIL

1 CARROT, MINCED

2 STALKS CELERY, MINCED

1/2 ONION, MINCED

4 CLOVES GARLIC, MINCED

1/2 TSP. SEA SALT

1/2 TSP. BLACK PEPPER

1 TSP. CHOPPED FRESH OREGANO

1 TSP. CHOPPED FRESH BASIL

1 TSP. CHOPPED FRESH PARSLEY

1/2 TSP. DRIED OREGANO

1 (28 OZ.) CAN DICED TOMATOES

1 (8 OZ.) CAN TOMATO SAUCE

1 (6 OZ.) CAN TOMATO PASTE

1/4 CUP CABERNET SAUVIGNON OR OTHER FULL-BODIED RED WINE

1 BAY LEAF

1. In a stockpot, warm the olive oil on medium-low heat for 1 minute, then add the carrot, celery, and onion (called a soffritto, the Italian mirepoix). Sauté until softened and the carrot starts to lose its color, about 5 minutes. Stir in the garlic, salt, pepper, fresh herbs, and dried oregano; sauté until aromatic, about 2 minutes. Add the remaining ingredients, raise the heat to medium, and bring to a simmer. Once simmering, reduce the heat to low and simmer for 2 hours, stirring every 20 minutes. Add water if the sauce gets too thick for your liking. Toss with rice pasta, vegetable noodles, or gnocchi (as pictured; recipe on page 112).

Variations:

• Add 1 tsp. chopped red chile peppers with the garlic and herbs to make a spicy arrabbiata sauce.

• Add 1 lb. ground beef, pork, sausage, or a beef/pork mixture to the soffritto (be sure to drain off most of the extra fat before adding the garlic and herbs) to make a Bolognese sauce.

• Add a can of chopped clams (juice included) when adding the tomatoes to make a more traditional marinara sauce.

• Add chopped mushrooms and/or zucchini slices with the garlic and herbs for texture.

• Add another 1 Tbsp. chopped fresh basil or oregano a few minutes before serving to make a more distinctly flavored sauce.

• Substitute 2 Tbsp. vodka for the red wine, and add ¼ cup heavy cream during the last few minutes of simmering to make a vodka sauce.

• Stir in 2 Tbsp. Simple Basil Pesto (page 54) or grated Parmesan cheese during the last few minutes of cooking for a little added tanginess.

• Gently blend the sauce with an immersion blender near the end of cooking to make a chunk-free sauce (which goes great on Pizza, page 122).

Simple Basil Pesto

The name pesto *comes from a Genoese (northern Italian) word that means "to crush" or "to pound," implying the use of a mortar and pestle. In fact, the English word* pestle *has the same root. While pastes have been used in Italy since the Roman era, basil wasn't introduced until later, from Africa (by way of India). The modern interpretation of basil pesto dates back only to the 19th century, with the paste gaining widespread popularity during the latter half of the 20th century.*

High-quality Parmesan or Pecorino (sheep's milk) cheese is the key to making a memorable pesto. Garlic scape, broccoli stems, watercress, and kale stalks can all be used to add fiber and a different tinge of flavor; just be sure to add more oil to offset the extra fiber.

YIELDS: 1 CUP
PREP TIME: 5 MINUTES

2 CUPS FRESH BASIL LEAVES

1/3 CUP PINE NUTS

3 CLOVES GARLIC

1/3 CUP OLIVE OIL

1/2 CUP GRATED AGED PARMIGIANO-REGGIANO OR PECORINO PEPATO CHEESE

1. Blend the basil and pine nuts in a blender or food processor, then add the garlic and blend again. Add the olive oil and cheese and blend one last time. Stir in more oil if the sauce is too thick. This pesto should last a few weeks in the fridge.

Uses for Simple Basil Pesto:

- Serve with Gnocchi (page 112).

- Use in place of tomato sauce when making Pizza (page 122).

- Mix into Pão de Queijo dough (page 121).

- Spoon into Basic Red Sauce (page 53) for extra flavor.

- Use as a marinade for grilled chicken breasts or thighs.

- Thin the paste with more oil and use as a salad dressing.

Guacamole

Guacamole was originally developed by the Aztecs. The word guacamole *is derived from the Aztec words for avocado and sauce (ahuacatl + molli) and dates back at least to the 1600s. In Mexico, the word is still pronounced like "wakamole," a remnant of its origin.*

My recipe is a typical baseline for this delicious condiment, but many variations exist. For example, in Venezuela a similar avocado-based sauce is made with vinegar and chile peppers. Common variations include adding a couple cloves of roasted garlic, some Preserved Lemons (page 61), or chopped bacon.

YIELDS: 2 1/2 CUPS
PREP TIME: 15 MINUTES

1 ROMA TOMATO, SEEDED AND FINELY CHOPPED

2 RIPE AVOCADOS, HALVED, PITS REMOVED

JUICE OF 1 LIME (2 TBSP.)

1/2 RED ONION, FINELY CHOPPED

1/4 CUP FRESH CILANTRO, CHOPPED

1/4 TSP. SEA SALT

1/4 TSP. BLACK PEPPER

1. Salt the chopped tomato and leave to drain in a colander for 10 minutes, then pat dry. This will add bite to the tomatoes and prevent the guacamole from getting watered down.

2. Scoop out the avocado flesh and roughly mash in a medium bowl. Mix in the rest of the ingredients, seasoning with salt to taste.

SAUCES, CONDIMENTS, AND OTHER BASICS

Harissa

Harissa is a North African chili sauce, commonly used as a condiment and curry base in Tunisia, Libya, Algeria, and Morocco. Its complex and slightly spicy taste is often compared to a similar Asian sauce, the equally delicious and almighty Sriracha. Harissa pairs well with many curry sauces, especially Lamb Tagine (page 160). While there is mention of harissa as early as the 13th century, it probably didn't take the form we recognize today until later, since chile peppers arrived in Europe and Africa following Columbus's discovery of the New World.

Piri Piri chiles (sometimes spelled peri peri or pili pili) are small, spicy peppers native to Africa. They are often compared to bird's eye chiles; in fact, they are sometimes called the "African bird's eye." Either type is fine for this recipe. If you can't find them, chile de árbol or even half a habañero chile will work; the point is to add a little heat to the milder dried chiles.

YIELDS: 1/4 CUP

PREP TIME: 30 MINUTES, PLUS 1 HOUR TO LET THE FLAVORS MARRY

---

4 LARGE DRIED MILD CHILES (ANAHEIM, NEW MEXICO, GUAJILLO, OR ANCHO)

1 SMALL HOT CHILE (PIRI PIRI, BIRD'S EYE, OR CHILE DE ÁRBOL, DRIED OR FRESH), SEEDS AND RIBS REMOVED

2 CLOVES GARLIC

1 TSP. SEA SALT

1 TSP. GROUND CUMIN

1 TSP. GROUND CORIANDER

1 TSP. CARAWAY SEEDS

1/4 CUP OLIVE OIL

1. Soak the dried chiles in warm water for 30 minutes, then remove the stems and seeds.

2. In a blender, blend all the ingredients to a smooth purée, then put it in the fridge to allow the flavors to marry for at least 1 hour. For best results, harissa should be eaten the next day, but it will keep for several weeks.

Guajillo

SAUCES, CONDIMENTS, AND OTHER BASICS

Preserved Lemons

YIELDS: 1 PINT
PREP TIME: 20 MINUTES
FERMENTATION TIME: 3-4 WEEKS

Lemons have been pickled for several hundred years, although the preserved lemons we know today were first documented in the 1800s. Preserved lemons retain their lemony taste without the intensity of fresh lemon.

4 LEMONS
1/3 CUP KOSHER SALT

1. Dip the lemons in nearly boiling water for 45 seconds. Slice the lemons into quarters and place in a large bowl. With your hands, thoroughly mix with half of the salt.

2. Line the bottom of a pint jar with salt, then tightly pack the lemon quarters into the jar, adding more salt with each layer. Cover the jar and let it sit in a cool, dark place for 3-4 weeks. Preserved lemons can be kept in the fridge for up to 6 months.

Uses for Preserved Lemons:

• Add to curries like Lamb Tagine (page 160) to add a fresh dynamic.

• Mince and add sparingly to Bloody Marys (along with their liquid).

• Mince and add to salad dressings.

• Chop and add to Guacamole (page 56) or homemade salsa.

Satay Sauce

Satay sauce is primarily a dipping sauce in the United States, but it takes on a different role in Southeast Asia, where it originated; in addition to being used as a dip, it is a general-purpose condiment used to provide depth to dishes and is the pivotal ingredient in many Indonesian dishes. It is also wildly popular in the Netherlands, a result of its colonization of Indonesia in the 17th-19th centuries.

While this dish is traditionally made with peanuts, I prefer to use a combination of walnuts, almonds, and macadamia nuts for a more ideal health benefit. Surprisingly, you can't really tell that there are no peanuts in this sauce—it's the combination of shrimp paste, garlic, coconut milk, and honey that gives this sauce its signature taste.

YIELDS: 1 CUP
PREP TIME: 5 MINUTES
COOKING TIME: 20 MINUTES

1 CUP TOTAL WALNUTS, ALMONDS, AND MACADAMIA NUTS

1 TSP. COCONUT OIL

1 TBSP. SHRIMP PASTE (TERASI PREFERRED; SEE PAGE 30)

1/2 BIRD'S EYE CHILE, SEEDS AND RIBS REMOVED, SLICED

2 CLOVES GARLIC, CHOPPED

1 TBSP. HONEY OR 2 TSP. COCONUT PALM SUGAR

1/2 TSP. SEA SALT

1/4 TSP. WHITE PEPPER

1 CUP COCONUT MILK

1. In a saucepan, toast the nuts on medium-low for 5 minutes, being careful not to burn, then set aside. In the same saucepan, heat the coconut oil on medium-low for 1 minute, then add the shrimp paste; toast until the oil starts to separate, about 3 minutes, then set aside to cool for 5 minutes.

2. In a blender or food processor, blend the nuts, shrimp paste mixture, and remaining ingredients until smooth. Return everything to the saucepan and simmer on medium heat until dark and thickened, 8-10 minutes. Add water to achieve the desired consistency; the sauce should be thick but pourable. Serve at room temperature. Leftover sauce will keep in the fridge for up to a week.

Teriyaki Sauce

Teriyaki sauce can be traced back to the Edo age in Japan, which started in the 17th century. An increase in urbanization and exposure to outside cultures resulted in an influx of new ingredients, which converged to make this tangy, sweet sauce that is perfect for grilling. Japanese restaurants gained prominence in the United States in the 1960s, and teriyaki sauce became the household name that it is today.

Because tamari is naturally bitter, it takes a fair amount of other tastes to balance everything. You might be surprised that it doesn't need much honey or other sweeteners—it's the presence of lime juice, fresh ginger, and white pepper that brings together the flavors.

YIELDS: 2 CUPS
PREP TIME: 5 MINUTES
COOKING TIME: 15 MINUTES

---

1 TBSP. ARROWROOT STARCH

1 TBSP. COLD WATER

1 1/3 CUPS CHICKEN BROTH (PAGE 42)

1/2 CUP TAMARI

1/4 CUP MIRIN (SWEET RICE WINE)

3 TBSP. HONEY

1 TSP. RICE VINEGAR

1 TSP. LIME JUICE

1 TSP. SESAME OIL

1/2" GINGER, PEELED AND MINCED OR GRATED

3 CLOVES GARLIC, MINCED

1/2 TSP. WHITE PEPPER

1. Combine the arrowroot starch with the cold water in a small bowl to form a slurry, then set aside. Combine the remaining ingredients in a saucepan, and bring to a simmer on low. Gently simmer for 10 minutes or until the flavors have married. Stir in the arrowroot slurry and continue to stir until the sauce thickens, about 5 minutes.

Variations:

Teriyaki is a very versatile sauce. Here are some of my favorite variations:

- **Ponzu sauce:** Omit the arrowroot starch and add 1 tsp. lemon juice.

- **Yakitori sauce:** Add 1 Tbsp. saké.

- **Gyoza/dipping sauce:** Omit the arrowroot starch, increase the rice vinegar to 1 Tbsp., and add a dash of chili powder and a few pinches of chopped scallions.

CHAPTER 3

VEGETABLES

Garlic Dill Pickles

Cucumbers have been pickled for more than 4,000 years. They were first grown in India before making their way to Europe, where they were paired with dill (originally from the Mediterranean). The healing properties of fermented vegetables were well known even several hundred years ago; Napoleon served pickles to his troops, and Columbus brought them on his travels to fight scurvy. Today, most pickles in the United States are made using vinegar, but traditional pickles were made with a simple brine. This recipe follows the traditional preparation.

Lactobacillus bacteria covers the skin of growing cucumbers and starts the fermentation process. It can be destroyed during commercial processing, so use organic cucumbers when available, or add ½ tsp. whey (the liquid that forms on top of yogurt) to the jar to kick-start the fermentation process.

SERVES: 4

PREP TIME: 30 MINUTES

FERMENTATION TIME: UP TO 10 DAYS

---

1 QUART FILTERED WATER

2 TBSP. SEA SALT

3 STALKS FRESH DILL, FLOWERS ATTACHED IF POSSIBLE

6 CLOVES GARLIC

1/4 TSP. WHITE MUSTARD SEEDS

1/4 TSP. BLACK PEPPERCORNS

2 OR 3 GRAPE LEAVES

3 OR 4 FRESH KIRBY CUCUMBERS, RINSED AND SLICED IN HALF LENGTHWISE

1. Bring the water to a boil and stir in the salt to dissolve. Allow to cool, about 1 hour. Line the bottom of a quart-sized jar with the dill, garlic, mustard seeds, peppercorns, and grape leaves. Carefully place the cut cucumbers in the jar, packing as many as can comfortably fit; do not overpack. Pour in the brine until the jar is nearly full; add a small ceramic dish or clean stone to weigh down the cucumbers.

2. Cover with a tight-fitting lid and store in a cool, dark place. Release air pressure by burping the lids every 2 days. Letting the pickles ferment for 4 days creates a "half-sour" pickle; "full-sour" pickles can ferment for up to 10 days. Be sure to spoon out any mold that forms on the top layer of the brine; there likely won't be any mold as long as the cucumbers are kept under the brine. Cloudiness is a good sign that indicates fermentation is happening.

3. Once the cucumbers are fermented to your liking, cover and refrigerate them for at least a day before eating. They should last for about a month in the fridge.

Kabees El Lift
(Pickled Turnips)

YIELDS: 8 CUPS (2 QUARTS)

PREP TIME: 30 MINUTES

FERMENTATION TIME: UP TO 7 DAYS

Kabees el lift is a popular Lebanese dish, often served as a lighter side to heavy meat dishes. It sports a vibrant pink color, which is made by adding beets to the turnips as they ferment. Turnips predate the Roman Empire and possibly ancient Greece. Beets are just as ancient, although they were originally cultivated for their greens; their bulbous roots were developed later.

Apple cider vinegar is not necessary for this recipe, but it creates a unique flavor profile. Using a simple salt brine creates a different probiotic profile. Adding 1 tsp. whey (the liquid that forms at the top of yogurt) aids in fermentation but also creates a unique probiotic profile. I've tried all three methods and they are all tasty; feel free to experiment.

1/4 CUP SEA SALT

2 LBS. TURNIPS (6 OR 7 TURNIPS)

2 SMALL BEETS (OR 1 MEDIUM BEET CUT IN HALF)

2 CLOVES GARLIC

2 BAY LEAVES

1/2 CUP APPLE CIDER VINEGAR

1. Dissolve the salt in 1 cup boiling water, then remove from the heat. Add 2 cups cold water, then let cool to room temperature, about 20 minutes. As the water cools, peel and slice the turnips into spears the size of large French fries, and peel the beets. Arrange the garlic, beets, turnips, and bay leaves in 2 quart-sized jars (1 garlic, 1 beet, and 1 bay leaf per jar) with tight-fitting lids. You can also use 1 half-gallon jar.

2. Add the vinegar to the cool water, stir, then pour the brine into your jars until there's about ½" air left in each jar. Weight down the vegetables with a small ceramic dish or clean stone. Cover the jars with their lids and let them sit in a cool, dark area of the house for at least 4 days or up to 7 days. Release air pressure by burping the lids every 2 days, and spoon out any mold that forms on the top layer of the brine; there likely won't be any mold as long as the vegetables are kept under the brine. Store in the fridge for up to 2 months.

Do Chua
(Vietnamese Pickled Daikon and Carrots)

Do chua is a traditional Vietnamese side dish and condiment that is often used as a relish. It's commonly served in sandwiches, added to salads, or served with grilled meat dishes. These pickled vegetables differ from other pickles in that they are often immediately refrigerated to retain their crunchy texture; I prefer to let mine sit at room temperature for four hours before putting them in the fridge to allow for a little fermentation.

YIELDS: 1 PINT

PREP TIME: 4 1/2 HOURS PLUS OVERNIGHT

COOKING TIME: 5 MINUTES

1 1/2 CUPS WATER

1 TBSP. SEA SALT

1 TBSP. HONEY

2 TBSP. RICE VINEGAR

1 LARGE CARROT (1/4 LB.)

1/2 SMALL DAIKON RADISH (1/4 LB.)

1. Bring the water to boil, then add the sea salt and honey, stirring until dissolved. Set aside to cool to room temperature, about 30 minutes. Once the brine has cooled, stir in the rice vinegar.

2. As the water cools, cut the carrot and daikon into matchstick-sized pieces. Gently squeeze and massage the carrot and daikon for about 2 minutes with your hands until they start to expel a little of their juices. Put the veggies and their juices in a pint-sized glass jar, packing in as many as possible. You should be able to get them all in, but if you can't, you could use the leftovers as a salad topping.

3. Pour the cooled brine over the veggies until the jar is full. Let it sit out at room temperature, uncovered and away from sunlight, for 4 hours. Cover and put in the fridge, allowing the flavors to marry overnight. Store in the fridge for up to a month. After opening up the jar, give the pickles 15 minutes to air out before eating; they are initially very smelly.

Kimchi

Kimchi is a major part of Korea's cultural identity, and for good cause: fermented vegetables were important for the survival of early Koreans. Because the Korean peninsula is especially cold in the winter, fermentation allowed Koreans to eat vegetables during the winter. Furthermore, fermented vegetables helped the early Koreans digest the first grains in their diet, which were barley and millet. Today, it's such an integral part of Korean culture that South Korea spent millions of dollars making an odor-free version that could be enjoyed onboard the Soyuz space station without disturbing the other astronauts.

Traditionally, kimchi is made in jars left to ferment underground for several months. The addition of red chili came after contact with Europeans, around the 17th century. Kimchi is most often made with won bok cabbage, but cucumber and daikon radish versions are also common.

YIELDS: 2 QUARTS
PREP TIME: 2 1/2 HOURS
FERMENTATION TIME: UP TO 1 WEEK

1-2 LBS. WON BOK (NAPA) CABBAGE

2 TBSP. SEA SALT

2 TBSP. FISH SAUCE

3 CLOVES GARLIC

1/2 SMALL ONION

1/4 PEAR OR ASIAN PEAR

1/2" GINGER, PEELED AND CHOPPED

3 TBSP. KOREAN RED PEPPER POWDER

2 TBSP. JULIENNED DAIKON RADISH

2 GREEN ONIONS, SLICED INTO 2" PIECES

1. Peel off and discard any damaged outer layers of the cabbage. Make a slice lengthwise through the center of the bottom third of the cabbage, then pull the 2 halves apart with your hands. This enables you to cut the cabbage in half lengthwise without damaging the leaves. Repeat with each half to cut the cabbage into quarters. Cut these quarters into 1½"-wide pieces, discarding the bottom inch (which looks more like a stem than leaves). Don't fret over cutting the kimchi exactly to specification; this is just how it's often cut in Korea.

2. Place the cabbage in a large bowl and fill with cold water; soak for 10 minutes, then rinse and strain in a colander. Set the colander over a bowl, then salt the cabbage and let it sit for 2 hours, rotating the cabbage every 30 minutes. Rinse thoroughly with cold water and allow to drain for 10 minutes.

3. Blend the fish sauce, garlic, onion, pear, and ginger, then mix in the Korean red pepper powder, daikon radish, and green onions. Put the cabbage in a large bowl, then mix in the red pepper powder mixture. Pack into 2 quart-sized jars, cover, and ferment at room temperature for at least 3 days or up to 1 week. Burp the lids at least once a day to prevent pressure buildup: it'll build up faster than you expect. If you forget to burp for a day or two, be sure to burp it in the sink to catch any pressurized juices. Store the kimchi in the fridge for up to a month.

Wedge Salad

SERVES: 4

PREP TIME: UP TO 24 HOURS

COOKING TIME: 20 MINUTES

While paying a restaurant chef money to simply quarter a head of lettuce and throw some toppings on it often feels ludicrous, I find the same technique to be both fun and easy on the wallet when done at home. Salads served wedge-style date back to the 1910s and reached peak popularity in the 1960s. Iceberg lettuce, the staple lettuce used in this dish, has slowly been replaced by leaf lettuces over the years, but I still have a soft spot in my heart for this crispy, blank-canvas lettuce; it stays fresher longer than leaf lettuces and pairs better with creamy dressings and heavier toppings, as in this recipe.

1/2 CUP SOUR CREAM

1/2 CUP MAYONNAISE (PAGE 50)

1/2 TBSP. WHITE WINE VINEGAR

1/2 TBSP. LEMON JUICE

1/2 TSP. GARLIC POWDER

1/2 TSP. ONION POWDER

4 OZ. CRUMBLED BLUE CHEESE, DIVIDED

SALT AND BLACK PEPPER TO TASTE

1 HEAD ICEBERG LETTUCE

20 GRAPE TOMATOES, SLICED IN HALF LENGTHWISE

4 RADISHES, THINLY SLICED

6 OZ. BACON, COOKED AND CHOPPED

1. In a bowl, whisk together the sour cream, mayonnaise, white wine vinegar, lemon juice, garlic powder, and onion powder. Stir in 2 oz. of the blue cheese and add salt and pepper to taste. The dressing can be used immediately, but for best results, cover and refrigerate it for up to 24 hours to let the flavors marry.

2. Core and quarter the head of lettuce, then top each wedge with dressing, tomatoes, radishes, bacon, and the remaining 2 oz. crumbled blue cheese.

Beet Salad
(Vinegret)

Vinegret is the name of a Russian salad that is likely not of Russian origin, but rather borrowed from German or Scandinavian cuisine. In traditional Russian cuisine, salads were pretty rare. Vinegret is often cited as the first Russian salad, first mentioned in the 19th century.

Another Russian favorite is Olivier salad, which has a much more interesting history. It was invented by Lucien Olivier, a Belgian chef working in Moscow in the 1860s. The original recipe was a closely held secret and was never truly duplicated. Documents reveal that the salad likely included caviar, crawfish tails, aspic, and veal tongue. Over the years, these rare ingredients were replaced by common ones. Instructions for making Olivier Salad are also found below, as the method is similar.

SERVES: 6

PREP TIME: 20 MINUTES

COOKING TIME: 40 MINUTES

---

2 MEDIUM BEETS

2 MEDIUM POTATOES, PEELED

3 CARROTS

1/2 CUP SAUERKRAUT, DRAINED

1/2 CUP GARLIC DILL PICKLES (PAGE 68), DICED

1 TBSP. OLIVE OIL

1/2 GREEN APPLE, DICED

1/2 TBSP. APPLE CIDER VINEGAR

1. Bring two pots of water to a boil. In one pot, gently boil the beets until they can be pierced with a fork, about 20 minutes; in the other, gently boil the potatoes until softened, about 10 minutes. Separately, steam the carrots until softened, about 8 minutes. Strain and rinse the vegetables and allow to cool. Once cool, peel and dice the beets into ½" chunks, using rubber gloves if you have them. Dice the potatoes and carrots into ½" chunks.

2. Combine the vegetables with the sauerkraut, dill pickles, oil, apple, and vinegar in a large stain-resistant bowl, and mix together with your hands or a large spoon until everything is bright red. This salad will keep for up to a week and tastes better the following day.

Variation:

For Olivier salad, omit the beets, olive oil, apple, and vinegar; replace with ½ cup diced ham, ½ cup hard-boiled eggs, ½ cup cooked peas, and ¼ cup Mayonnaise (page 50). Add crawfish tails if desired.

Cauliflower Rice

Cauliflower rice is a low-carb solution for those wanting a rice-like texture without eating actual rice. It fares best when covered in a curry or other sauce. Cauliflower rice can be fried but needs to be added at the very end of cooking at a high temperature for only a couple minutes.

Cauliflower has probably existed for more than 2,000 years; it is believed to have originally come from Cyprus. Cauliflower is a direct descendant of wild cabbage and a close cousin to broccoli. Although it was known in Europe during the Middle Ages, it disappeared until sometime in the 17th century, when Italy reintroduced it to the French, who spread it throughout the rest of Europe sometime thereafter.

SERVES: 4

PREP TIME: 5 MINUTES

COOKING TIME: 10 MINUTES

1 HEAD CAULIFLOWER, COARSELY CHOPPED

1 TBSP. BUTTER OR COCONUT OIL

1 TBSP. WATER

SALT TO TASTE

1. Add the chopped cauliflower to a food processor and pulse until it is the consistency of rice or couscous.

2. In a large skillet, warm the butter or coconut oil on medium heat for 1 minute, then stir in the cauliflower. Sauté until sizzling, then add the water, cover, reduce the heat to low, and simmer until softened, about 7 minutes. Season with salt to taste and either serve or let cool for use in other dishes.

Bibimbap

Bibimbap is a traditional Korean dish that's a lot of fun to say aloud. Legend has it that the dish originated from the belief that leftover food cannot be brought into the New Year. For that reason, Koreans started the practice of mixing together various ingredients in one bowl.

There is an unlimited amount of variability to this dish and many regional specialties. The most popular version is dolsot bibimbap, which is plated in a hot stoneware bowl, cooking the outside layer of rice into a crunchy, delicious treat.

The ingredients listed below should be treated as just a suggestion of the wide variety you can add to this dish. Consider this dish like Congee (page 106) or Fried Rice (page 104)—a tasty way of finishing off leftovers.

Boiled royal fern can be found packaged in Asian markets.

SERVES: 4

PREP TIME: 30 MINUTES, PLUS TIME TO PREP THE RICE AND KALBI

COOKING TIME: 10 MINUTES TO FRY EGGS AND ARRANGE DISHES

2 TSP. COCONUT OIL, DIVIDED

1 CUP BOILED ROYAL FERN (GOBI NAMUL), SLICED INTO 3" LENGTHS

3 CLOVES GARLIC, MINCED, DIVIDED

2 TSP. SESAME OIL, DIVIDED

1 CUP RAW SPINACH

2 CUPS WARM COOKED WHITE RICE (PAGE 96)

1 CUP DO CHUA (PAGE 71)

1 CUP KIMCHI (PAGE 72)

1 CUP WARM COOKED KALBI (PAGE 146)

4 EGGS

2 TSP. SESAME SEEDS TO GARNISH

KOCHUJANG SAUCE (BELOW)

1. In a small saucepan, heat 1 tsp. of the coconut oil on medium heat for 1 minute, then add the boiled fern and half of the garlic. Sauté until warmed, about 2 minutes, then remove from the heat, toss with 1 tsp. of the sesame oil, and set aside. Sauté the spinach and the rest of the garlic in the remaining 1 tsp. coconut oil, adding 1 Tbsp. water after 1 minute of sautéing to help blanch it. Toss in the remaining 1 tsp. sesame oil and set aside.

2. The same process can be used for other vegetables, like sliced cucumber, shiitake mushrooms, grated carrots, or daikon radish. Place the cooked veggies in the fridge to cool for 20 minutes.

3. Distribute and pack the white rice in the bottoms of 4 bowls. Arrange the meat and veggies in sections around each bowl, then fry the eggs and place one in each bowl. Garnish with sesame seeds. Serve with any leftover garnishes and kochujang sauce (see recipe below).

KOCHUJANG (OR GOCHUJANG) SAUCE

2 TBSP. KOREAN RED PEPPER POWDER

2 CLOVES GARLIC

1 TBSP. RICE VINEGAR

1 TSP. TAMARI

1 TSP. SESAME OIL

2 TSP. HONEY

3 TBSP. CHICKEN BROTH (PAGE 42)

1. Blend the sauce ingredients, then add salt to taste. Serve at room temperature.

Chinese Greens

SERVES: 4

PREP TIME: 5 MINUTES

COOKING TIME: 15 MINUTES

There are a wide and tasty variety of Chinese greens in China, many of which are commonly found in Western markets today. Typical cabbage greens like kale, collards, and chard require extended cooking times, but Chinese greens are often sautéed at high temperatures for a short time, then garnished with a flavorful sauce. For more information on Chinese greens, see page 30.

1/3 CUP CHICKEN BROTH (PAGE 42)

2 TBSP. CHINESE COOKING WINE (SEE PAGE 30)

1/4 TSP. WHITE PEPPER

SALT TO TASTE

1 TSP. ARROWROOT STARCH OR POTATO STARCH

1 TSP. COLD WATER

1 LB. WHOLE LEAFY CHINESE GREENS, LIKE CHOY SUM, KAI-LAN, OR BOK CHOY

1 TBSP. COCONUT OIL

1" GINGER, PEELED AND GRATED

1. Combine the chicken broth, Chinese cooking wine, and white pepper, adding salt to taste; set aside. Mix together the starch and cold water in a small bowl and set aside.

2. Rinse the greens in cold water, then drain. Bring a stockpot of water to a boil, dip the greens into the water using tongs, and blanch for 30 seconds. Drain and rinse the greens with cold water, then set aside.

3. Heat the oil in a wok on high heat until shimmering, about 1 minute. Add the ginger and sauté until aromatic, 15-30 seconds. Add the greens and sauce and simmer until the greens are wilted, about 2 minutes. Remove the greens with tongs and place in a serving dish, keeping the sauce in the wok. Add the starch slurry to the sauce, stirring until thickened, about 1 minute. Pour the thickened sauce over the greens and serve.

Roasted Root Vegetables

Root vegetables were important at many different times during human history. It's believed that they were vital foods during human evolution. They were also favored in early empires, as they kept well over cold winters. Root vegetables were important staples until the rise of grains and agriculture in the early Neolithic period. Settlers in North America relied heavily on root vegetables for survival during the early years of settlement.

This dish isn't limited to the ingredients listed below; feel free to experiment with other root vegetables, like potatoes, turnips, celery root, Jerusalem artichokes, and kohlrabi bulbs (all cut to similar sizes).

SERVES: 6
PREP TIME: 10 MINUTES
COOKING TIME: 1 HOUR

5 CARROTS, SLICED IN HALF LENGTHWISE

5 PARSNIPS, SLICED IN HALF LENGTHWISE

4 LARGE BEETS, PEELED AND QUARTERED

1 HEAD GARLIC, SEPARATED

8 SPRIGS FRESH THYME (OR 1/2 TSP. DRIED THYME)

2 TBSP. DUCK FAT, LARD, OR OLIVE OIL

1/2 TSP. SEA SALT

1/2 TSP. BLACK PEPPER

1. Preheat the oven to 400°F. Scatter the vegetables, garlic, and thyme on a rimmed baking sheet. Drizzle with melted fat or oil and sprinkle with salt and pepper.

2. Bake until fork-tender, about 1 hour, flipping the vegetables after 30 minutes.

Onion Rings

SERVES: 4

PREP TIME: 30 MINUTES

COOKING TIME: 20 MINUTES

Onion rings are a relatively new invention, with their first documentation appearing in the 19th century. They were popularized by A&W restaurants in the 1960s and are found in nearly every diner and fast-food chain today.

This starch-and-egg batter works well with other vegetables and creates a tempura-style texture. Try it with sliced carrots, zucchini, steamed sweet potato, broccoli, mushrooms, and roasted pumpkin.

2 LARGE SPANISH OR SWEET ONIONS, CUT INTO 1/4" ROUNDS AND SEPARATED INTO RINGS

1/4 CUP PLUS 1 TBSP. TAPIOCA STARCH, DIVIDED

1 CUP LARD

1/4 CUP POTATO STARCH OR ARROWROOT STARCH (OR A COMBINATION)

2 EGGS, BEATEN

1/2 TSP. SEA SALT

1/4 TSP. PAPRIKA OR CAYENNE PEPPER

1. Soak the onion rings in cold water for 30 minutes to reduce the astringency, then pat dry and lightly dust with 1 Tbsp. tapioca starch. Warm the lard in a skillet on medium-high heat; the ideal temperature is around 360°F. Combine the remaining ingredients and stir in cold water until the mixture reaches a batter-like consistency.

2. For frying, rapidly stir the batter, then quickly and carefully dip in a few onion rings. Pull from the batter and allow the excess to run off, then quickly insert into the lard to fry.

3. Flip when golden, after about 1 minute, then fry for 1 more minute. Drain on paper towels and season with salt to taste while still hot. Repeat the process until all the onions are fried.

Saag Paneer

Saag paneer is an Indian dish of greens and fresh cheese. Like many traditional dishes, it is a combination of regional ingredients and timing.

Saag is an ancient dish whose main ingredients (turmeric, mustard seeds, and greens) date back to 3000 BC. In the Indus Valley, cattle were domesticated in 7000 BC, but cheese-making came much later; legend has it that Mongols carrying leather bags of milk created it by happenstance—friction and heat turned the milk to cheese. Sometime later it was incorporated into Indian cuisine.

While mustard greens are the traditional greens used in this dish, many restaurants today make it with spinach. I find that a combination of the two strikes a nice balance between bitter and mild greens.

SERVES: 4

PREP TIME: 15 MINUTES, PLUS TIME TO PREP THE PANEER CHEESE

COOKING TIME: 40 MINUTES

1 ONION
1/4 TSP. TURMERIC
1/2" GINGER, PEELED
4 CLOVES GARLIC
2 TBSP. GHEE, DIVIDED
1/2 TSP. BLACK MUSTARD SEEDS
1 TSP. CUMIN SEEDS
1/2 LB. MUSTARD GREENS, COARSELY CHOPPED
1/2 LB. SPINACH, COARSELY CHOPPED
1/2 CUP WATER
1/2 TSP. GARAM MASALA
1/2 TSP. KASHMIRI RED CHILI POWDER
SALT TO TASTE
PANEER CHEESE (BELOW)

1. In a blender, process the onion, turmeric, ginger, and garlic into a smooth paste. In a large skillet, warm 1 Tbsp. of the ghee on medium heat until shimmering, then add the mustard and cumin seeds. Toast until the mustard seeds make a popping sound, about 5 minutes. Add the onion paste and sauté until aromatic and browned, about 8 minutes. Add the mustard greens, spinach, and water; stir, cover, and simmer on low until the greens have softened, about 20 minutes. Stir in the garam masala and chili powder and season with salt to taste.

2. As the saag simmers, warm the remaining 1 Tbsp. ghee in a skillet on medium heat and brown the paneer cheese cubes, in batches if needed, about 2 minutes per side. Drain on paper towels. Add the browned cheese to the saag, cover, and simmer for 3 more minutes; then serve.

PANEER CHEESE

SERVES: 4   **COOKING TIME:** 5 MINUTES   **PREP TIME:** 3 HOURS

4 CUPS WHOLE MILK
2 TBSP. WHITE VINEGAR OR LEMON JUICE
1/4 TSP. SEA SALT
1 TBSP. GHEE

1. Warm the milk on medium-high heat, stirring constantly, until just about to boil. Add the vinegar or lemon juice, reduce the heat to medium, and continue to stir until small curds form, about 45 seconds. Pour the milk into a colander lined with 4 layers of cheesecloth. Gently rinse the curds with cold water to remove the foam and excess whey; carefully stir in the salt.

2. Tie the cheesecloth at its corners and squeeze out as much liquid as possible. Tie the corners around a wooden spoon and suspend over a bowl for 1½ hours. Untie from the spoon, keeping the cheese in the cheesecloth, and press evenly between 2 plates until about 1" thick. Weight down the top plate with cans of food, then transfer to the fridge for 1 hour to finish.

3. Unwrap and slice the cheese into 1" cubes using a sharp, wet knife. Be sure to wipe the knife clean with a wet towel after every slice.

Cream of Mushroom Soup

The exact origin of cream of mushroom soup is unclear, but both soups and mushrooms have been around since antiquity. The French and Italians in particular have a long-standing history of preparing creamy soups. There is record of mushroom soups in the United States well before Campbell's Soups introduced its premade version in 1934, but the soup became wildly popular in the 1930s and beyond, to the point where it is often called "America's béchamel."

While white mushrooms make logical sense when crafting the recipe, robust, full-flavored mushrooms like the woodsy porcini and smoky shiitake greatly enhance the overall taste. If cost is a factor, you can substitute 1 ounce dried oyster mushrooms for the porcini.

SERVES: 4

PREP TIME: 40 MINUTES

COOKING TIME: 1 HOUR

1 OZ. DRIED PORCINI MUSHROOMS

1 LB. (16 OZ.) FRESH SHIITAKE MUSHROOMS, THINLY SLICED (OR 4 OZ. DRIED)

1/4 CUP OLIVE OIL

1 ONION, FINELY CHOPPED

3 CLOVES GARLIC, MINCED

2 SPRIGS FRESH ROSEMARY, COARSELY CHOPPED

4 FRESH SAGE LEAVES, COARSELY CHOPPED

6 CUPS CHICKEN BROTH (PAGE 42)

1 CUP HEAVY CREAM

2 TBSP. BUTTER

SALT AND WHITE PEPPER TO TASTE

1. Soak the porcini mushrooms in 1 cup warm water for 30 minutes; strain and reserve the soaking liquid. If using dried shiitake, soak them together with the porcini in 3 cups warm water. Slice the mushrooms into thin strips.

2. Heat the olive oil in a large stockpot on medium heat for 1 minute, then add the onion and sauté until softened, about 5 minutes. Add the garlic and herbs and sauté until aromatic, about 1 minute, then add the porcini and shiitake mushrooms. Sauté until softened, about 10 minutes.

3. Add the chicken broth and reserved soaking liquid. (If you used dried shiitake, pour in all the soaking liquid and only 4 cups chicken broth.) Bring to a simmer, reduce the heat to low, and simmer for 30 minutes. Using an immersion blender, purée the soup until smooth. Alternatively, you can blend it in batches in a blender.

4. Stir in the cream and butter and return to a simmer, then add salt and white pepper to taste. Remove from the heat and serve.

French Onion Soup

SERVES: 4

PREP TIME: 10 MINUTES

COOKING TIME: 2 HOURS

Onion soups were eaten by the ancient Greeks, but the French combination of caramelized onions, bread, and cheese was developed in the 17th century. Originally considered a lower-class food, French onion soup grew to popularity in the United States during the 1960s, like many French dishes.

2 TBSP. BUTTER

3 YELLOW ONIONS, HALVED AND THINLY SLICED INTO HALF-MOONS

1/2 TSP. SEA SALT

1/4 CUP DRY RED WINE

3 CUPS CHICKEN BROTH (PAGE 42)

2 CUPS BEEF BROTH (PAGE 42)

1/2 TSP. APPLE CIDER VINEGAR

1 SPRIG FRESH PARSLEY

1 SPRIG FRESH THYME

1 BAY LEAF

SALT AND BLACK PEPPER TO TASTE

1/2 LB. GRATED SWISS CHEESE, LIKE GRUYÈRE

1. Melt the butter in a stockpot on medium-low heat for 1 minute, then add the onions and salt. Sauté without stirring for 10 minutes, then stir and sauté until golden brown, about 50 minutes, stirring every 10 minutes and reducing the heat as needed to prevent burning. Add the wine and simmer until most of the wine has evaporated, about 10 minutes. Add the broths, vinegar, and herbs (tie them together in a bouquet garni or wrap them in cheesecloth). Simmer for 20 minutes, season with salt and pepper to taste, and discard the herbs.

2. Set the oven to broil for 5 minutes to preheat it. Ladle the soup into 4 bowls, then top with the grated Swiss cheese. Be sure to spread the cheese evenly so that it doesn't sink when it cooks. Place the bowls on a baking sheet and carefully place in the oven. Broil until the cheese is melted and browned, about 3 minutes, then carefully remove, let sit for 5 minutes, and serve.

3. For maximum flavor, refrigerate the soup overnight and reheat in a stockpot before ladling into bowls and topping with cheese.

CHAPTER 4
STARCHES

Basic Rice Recipes

Most people (including me) use rice cookers, but I find that cooking a pot of rice on the stove is a rewarding experience of its own. I make two main types of plain rice at home: medium-grain (calrose) rice is an excellent everyday rice, while long-grain basmati rice is fragrant and tends not to stick together. In all cases, white rice is preferred over brown rice (for more information, see page 26).

The methods for cooking these rices differ, but both types should be used as vessels for other nutrients. I like to boil medium-grain rice in broth and to steam basmati rice in coconut milk, butter, and spices.

BASIC STEAMED RICE

SERVES: 6

PREP TIME: 5 MINUTES

COOKING TIME: 40 MINUTES

---

2 CUPS MEDIUM-GRAIN (CALROSE) WHITE RICE

2 1/2 CUPS WATER OR CHICKEN BROTH (PAGE 42)

1. Rinse the rice until the water runs clear, about 3-4 changes of water, then drain and place in a stockpot. Add the water or broth and let the rice soak for 10 minutes. Cover and bring to a boil over high heat without lifting the lid, which should take about 5 minutes; listen for sounds of water boiling or the lid rattling.

2. Once it starts boiling, reduce the heat to low and simmer until the rice starts to make a hissing sound, which indicates that the water has evaporated, about 10-15 minutes. Turn the heat to high for 30 seconds to dry out the bottom of the rice, then turn off the heat. Leave the pot covered for 10 more minutes, then uncover and fluff the rice with a spoon or paddle.

STEAMED BASMATI RICE

SERVES: 6

PREP TIME: 5 MINUTES

COOKING TIME: 50 MINUTES, PLUS UP TO 6 HOURS TO SOAK THE RICE

---

2 CUPS LONG-GRAIN (BASMATI) RICE

2 QUARTS WATER

1 TBSP. COCONUT OIL

1 LARGE POTATO, CUT INTO 1/4" SLICES

2 TBSP. BUTTER OR GHEE

1/4 CUP COCONUT MILK

1/2 TSP. TURMERIC

1. Soak the rice in cold water for at least 1 hour or up to 6 hours. Rinse the rice until the water runs clear, then pour the rice into a stockpot and fill with 2 quarts water. Bring to a boil, reduce the heat, and gently simmer until the rice starts to float, about 6 minutes; strain and set aside. Spoon the coconut oil into the empty pot, then line the bottom of the pot with the potato slices. Using a large spoon, scoop the rice from the strainer into the pot, one scoop on top of the other, to make a conical shape. Do not tap or shake the pot, which will cause the rice to compact.

2. In a small saucepan, melt the butter or ghee, then stir it into the coconut milk and turmeric. Once combined, pour the mixture evenly over the rice in a spiral pattern. Wrap a towel or other cloth around the lid of the pot, clipping the excess cloth to the lid's handle.

3. Cover and steam the rice over medium heat for 7 minutes, then reduce the heat to low and steam for another 40 minutes. Uncover and gently stir the rice to distribute the turmeric.

4. In addition to or in place of the turmeric and coconut milk, feel free to experiment with other spices, including cumin seeds, dried cilantro, and saffron.

Sticky Rice

If you've eaten at a Thai restaurant, you've probably had sticky rice. In many parts of Southeast Asia (Laos and northern Thailand, for example), eating with your hands is still an accepted practice. Recent research has shown that ancient buildings in China used stones bound together by a sticky rice glue.

Sticky rice is also referred to as glutinous rice, but that doesn't mean it contains gluten—it simply refers to its glue-like texture. It is also labeled as sweet rice or mochi rice. It comes in short-grain and long-grain varieties; either type is fine.

SERVES: 4

PREP TIME: 2 HOURS (TO SOAK THE RICE)

COOKING TIME: 30 MINUTES

1 CUP SWEET, MOCHI, OR GLUTINOUS RICE (THEY'RE ALL THE SAME THING)

1. Soak the rice in cold water for 2 hours. Drain and rinse the rice, then put it in a metal colander; place the colander on top of a stockpot filled with at least 2" water. Cover the colander with a lid that's wrapped in a towel. Bring the water to a boil and steam for 10 minutes, then flip the rice with a spatula and steam until cooked through and opaque, about 5 more minutes.

2. Serve with a curry (like Chicken Panang, page 203) or use as a base for a dessert: for example, pair it with coconut milk and fresh fruit, like sliced mango.

Dirty Rice

Dirty rice is a Cajun dish made "dirty" by being cooked with chicken offal, usually a combination of livers, hearts, and gizzards. An essential part of this dish is its use of the "holy trinity" of Cajun cuisine: a mirepoix of onion, bell pepper, and celery.

Cajun cuisine is the product of French-speaking Acadian immigrants who were forced by the British to move from Acadia (eastern Canada) to Louisiana in the middle of the 18th century. Though similar, Cajun cuisine shouldn't be confused with Creole cuisine; while both use regionally available ingredients, Cajun cuisine is based almost exclusively on French culinary methods, while Creole cuisine takes cues from many European cooking methods.

It is easiest to mince chicken livers when they are partially frozen.

SERVES: 6

PREP TIME: 20 MINUTES

COOKING TIME: 1 HOUR

2 TBSP. BUTTER

1 SMALL ONION, DICED

1 GREEN BELL PEPPER, DICED

2 STALKS CELERY, DICED

2 CLOVES GARLIC, MINCED

1 LB. MIXED CHICKEN LIVERS AND GIBLETS (GIZZARDS AND HEARTS), MINCED

4 SAUSAGES (ANDOUILLE OR CHORIZO), SLICED AND QUARTERED

1 1/2 CUPS MEDIUM-GRAIN (CALROSE) WHITE RICE

1 TSP. CUMIN

1 TSP. PAPRIKA

1 TSP. SEA SALT

1 TSP. BLACK PEPPER

1/2 TSP. DRIED OREGANO

1/2 TSP. DRIED THYME

3 CUPS CHICKEN OR PORK STOCK (PAGE 42)

TABASCO TO TASTE

1 SMALL HANDFUL FRESH PARSLEY, CHOPPED

1. In a large skillet, warm the butter on medium heat, then add the onion, bell pepper, and celery and sauté until softened, about 4 minutes. Add the garlic and sauté for another minute, then add the minced chicken livers and giblets. Sauté for another 4 minutes, then add the sausages, rice, seasonings, and herbs. Toast the rice until opaque, stirring frequently, about 4 minutes.

2. Once the rice is toasted, stir in the stock and add 4 squirts of Tabasco. Bring to a boil, cover, reduce the heat to low, and simmer until the liquid evaporates, about 40 minutes. You'll know that the stock has been absorbed when the rice starts to make a hissing sound.

3. Uncover, stir in the parsley, and add salt, pepper, and Tabasco to taste.

4. This rice pairs perfectly with Southern Fried Chicken (page 194) and Meaty Collard Greens (page 172).

Mexican Rice

SERVES: 6
PREP TIME: 5 MINUTES
COOKING TIME: 1 HOUR

Mexican rice hails from northern Mexico and is often called Spanish rice despite the fact that it's not of Spanish origin. Rice was introduced to the Americas by the Spanish in the 16th century, which has been cited as the origin of this misnomer.

This recipe serves as a template for other rice dishes. To add more variety and color to the dish, add chopped onion, bell peppers, or precooked meats to the rice as it toasts.

1 (8 OZ.) CAN TOMATO SAUCE

2 CUPS CHICKEN BROTH (PAGE 42)

1 TSP. SEA SALT

1/2 TSP. BLACK PEPPER

1 TBSP. BUTTER

2 CUPS MEDIUM-GRAIN (CALROSE) WHITE RICE

1 CLOVE GARLIC, MINCED

1. Combine the tomato sauce, broth, salt, and pepper in a bowl and set aside; the total liquid amount should be near 2½ cups.

2. In a large skillet, warm the butter on medium-low heat for 1 minute, then add the rice and toast, stirring often, until opaque, about 8 minutes. Add the garlic and sauté until aromatic, about 1 minute. Add the sauce mixture to the skillet and turn up the heat to medium. Bring to a simmer, then cover and reduce the heat to low. Cook for 50 minutes or until the rice makes a sizzling sound near the bottom of the skillet. Remove from the heat and leave covered for 5 minutes before serving.

Fried Rice

Fried rice is the ultimate way to get rid of leftovers; all it takes is a little oil, rice, and ingenuity. Like Congee (page 106), fried rice has probably been around as long as people have been eating rice. This recipe is a solid baseline for making fried rice and can be expanded as desired.

Using a wok over a hot flame is the easiest way to make fried rice. I own a portable butane gas grill just for such occasions.

SERVES: 4

PREP TIME: 10 MINUTES

COOKING TIME: 10 MINUTES

2 EGGS

2 TBSP. COCONUT OIL, DIVIDED

1/2 LB. LEFTOVER COOKED MEAT (SUCH AS PORK ADOBO, PAGE 174)

2 CUPS COLD COOKED RICE (PAGE 96)

2 CARROTS, DICED

8 WON BOK CABBAGE LEAVES, SLICED

2 TSP. TAMARI

1 TSP. FISH SAUCE

1/2 TSP. SEA SALT

1/2 TSP. WHITE PEPPER

1 TSP. COCONUT PALM SUGAR

1 TSP. SESAME OIL

2 SPRING ONIONS, SLICED

1. Scramble the eggs until almost done, then set aside. Heat 1 Tbsp. of the coconut oil in a wok on medium-high heat until shimmering, then add the meat. Sauté until browned, stirring often with a wooden spoon, then remove from the pan and set aside.

2. Increase the heat to high and add the remaining 1 Tbsp. coconut oil. Heat until shimmering; then add the rice, breaking up any chunks. Fry, turning the rice every 30 seconds, until the grains start to brown around the edges, about 3-5 minutes. Add more oil if the rice gets too dry, but use oil sparingly.

3. Add the carrots, cabbage, tamari, fish sauce, salt, white pepper, and coconut palm sugar; stir-fry until everything is evenly coated. Continue to stir-fry until the cabbage wilts and softens, about 2 minutes. Add the sesame oil, meat, and eggs, turning off the heat. Add more salt and pepper to taste, then garnish with spring onions and serve.

Variations:

The possible variations of fried rice are endless. Favorites at my house include:

• Kimchi (page 72) Fried Rice with leftover Kalbi (page 146)

• Lemongrass Pork Chops (page 179) Fried Rice

• Jerk Pork (page 186) Fried Rice

• Barbecue Brisket (page 138) Fried Rice drizzled with Barbecue Sauce (page 48)

Congee

Humans have consumed rice for at least 4,000 years, and I would wager that rice porridge (commonly called congee in South Asia and juk in East Asia) has been around just as long. After all, it's basically just overcooked rice. It's been valued for centuries as a hearty source of calories that is easy to digest—it's often served to people when they are sick. It's also one of the most popular breakfast dishes on the planet.

While plain rice porridge isn't the most nutrient-dense food in the world, the simple truth is that congee has probably saved many populations from starvation throughout history. Adding a nutrient-dense chicken broth increases its nutritional profile significantly.

SERVES: 6

PREP TIME: 40 MINUTES

COOKING TIME: 4 HOURS

1 WHOLE CHICKEN (PASTURED CHICKEN OR STEWING HEN PREFERRED)

1/2 TSP. KOSHER SALT

1 GALLON WATER

1 CUP MEDIUM-GRAIN (CALROSE) WHITE RICE

1" FRESH GINGER, PEELED AND SLICED INTO STALKS

4 TBSP. CHINESE COOKING WINE (SEE PAGE 30)

1 TBSP. FISH SAUCE

2 OZ. DRIED MUSHROOMS (OYSTER, SHIITAKE, WOOD EAR, OR A COMBINATION)

1 TBSP. SEA SALT

1 TSP. WHITE PEPPER

4 GREEN ONIONS, SLICED

1. Remove the skin from the chicken (except from the wings) and cut away any large pieces of fat that are left. Sprinkle the kosher salt on the chicken and let it sit for 30 minutes, then rinse off the salt and thoroughly wash the chicken.

2. Bring the water to a boil in a large pot on high heat, then add the chicken; once it starts to boil again, reduce the heat to medium-low and gently simmer for 2 hours, uncovered, skimming foam and fat from the surface of the water as it accumulates. Add water to replace any that evaporates.

3. Rinse the rice until the water runs clear, then soak for 1 hour while the chicken simmers. Once the chicken has boiled for 2 hours, add the rice, ginger, cooking wine, and fish sauce. Partially cover the pot and simmer for another 30 minutes, then pull out the chicken with tongs and set aside to cool. Once the chicken has cooled, pull off the meat, shred it, and set it aside.

4. Continue to simmer the rice for another hour, again partially covered, stirring every 10 minutes so that the rice doesn't stick to the bottom of the pot. Soak the mushrooms in warm water for 30 minutes, then slice them into bite-sized chunks and add them to the pot of rice during the last 30 minutes of simmering.

5. Once the porridge has started to thicken and it's hard to see individual grains of rice, you're ready to check it for taste. At this point, it'll be pretty bland, so add salt and white pepper until it tastes delicious. Once you're happy with the taste, turn off the heat, cover, and let it sit for 10 minutes to thicken some more. After 10 minutes, spoon it into individual bowls and garnish with the shredded chicken and green onions.

Garlic Mashed Potatoes

Potatoes were brought to Europe from the New World (specifically the Andes) in the 16th century, but mashed potatoes were first documented in the 18th century. Something akin to mashed potatoes was likely eaten by indigenous Americans before then, but no record exists today.

Potatoes mashed with just cream and butter are delicious on their own, but taking the extra step of roasting garlic beforehand brings it to another level and is worth the invested time.

SERVES: 6

PREP TIME: 1 HOUR (TO ROAST THE GARLIC)

COOKING TIME: 20 MINUTES

1 HEAD GARLIC, TOP 1/4" CHOPPED OFF AND DISCARDED

1 TBSP. OLIVE OIL

2 LBS. RUSSET OR YUKON GOLD POTATOES, PEELED AND CUT INTO 1" CHUNKS

4 TBSP. BUTTER, CUBED

1/2 TBSP. SEA SALT

1 TSP. BLACK PEPPER

~1/2 CUP HEAVY CREAM

1. Preheat the oven to 350°F. Place the garlic on a sheet of aluminum foil, drizzle with the olive oil, and loosely wrap into a teardrop shape. Roast for 45 minutes, then check for doneness by squeezing the sides of the garlic, which should be soft. Squeeze out the garlic cloves and set aside.

2. As the garlic finishes roasting, prepare the potatoes. Put them in a large stockpot and fill with enough cold water to cover the potatoes by 1". Bring to a boil on high heat, reduce the heat to medium, and simmer until fork-tender, about 15 minutes.

3. Strain the potatoes and return them to the stockpot; stir in the butter, salt, pepper, and garlic and mash with a hand masher or whisk until well mixed and fluffy, stirring in as much cream as needed to get your desired consistency (about ½ cup). Be careful not to overmash, which will result in glue-like potatoes. Add more salt and pepper to taste if desired.

Colcannon

Although potato and kale recipes are found all over Europe, the Irish variation, colcannon, is granddaddy of them all. The Romans introduced cabbage to most of Europe but were surprised to find that cabbage was already in Ireland when they arrived. The Celts are generally recognized as having brought cabbage to Ireland, nearly 500 years before the Roman Empire rose to power.

Although potatoes weren't introduced to Europe until the 1500s, the Irish were one of the first peoples to embrace them, and it is safe to assume that colcannon followed shortly thereafter.

Colcannon is usually treated as a St. Patrick's Day dish in the United States, but it is traditionally a Halloween dish in Ireland. Historically, some families would put a plate of colcannon outside their front door with a large chunk of butter in the middle to feed ghosts and fairies that were passing by.

This dish goes especially well with sausages, which can be pan-fried or grilled while the potatoes are simmering.

SERVES: 6

PREP TIME: 10 MINUTES

COOKING TIME: 30 MINUTES

2 LBS. RUSSET OR YUKON GOLD POTATOES, PEELED AND CUT INTO 1" CHUNKS

6 TBSP. BUTTER, CUBED

1/2 CUP CHOPPED LEEK OR GREEN ONIONS

1 BUNCH KALE (ABOUT 6 STALKS), STEMS REMOVED, COARSELY CHOPPED

1/2 CUP HEAVY CREAM

SALT AND BLACK PEPPER TO TASTE, ~1/2 TSP. EACH

1. Place the potatoes in a stockpot, then fill with enough water to cover the potatoes by 1". Bring to a boil on high heat, then reduce the heat to medium and simmer until fork-tender, about 15 minutes. Drain the potatoes in a colander and leave them there as you prep the other ingredients.

2. Add the butter to the empty stockpot and warm on medium heat. Add the leek or green onions and simmer until aromatic, about 1 minute. Add the kale and sauté until bright green, about 3 minutes. Add the potatoes and cream, remove from the heat, and mash everything together until well mixed. Season with salt and pepper to taste. Serve with sausage and an extra dollop of butter on top.

Gnocchi

Gnocchi are a type of dumpling most often made with potatoes. Like many Italian recipes, there is a lot of variability to the dish. It's believed that gnocchi have been around since the Roman era and that they actually came from the Middle East. It's unclear whether the word gnocchi *comes from* nocchio *(a knot in wood) or from* nocca *(knuckle).*

Prior to the arrival of potatoes from the New World, semolina (coarse-ground durum wheat) was used to make gnocchi; semolina gnocchi recipes are still around today.

SERVES: 6

PREP TIME: 2 HOURS (TO BAKE AND COOL THE POTATOES)

COOKING TIME: 30 MINUTES

3 LARGE RUSSET POTATOES (ABOUT 2 LBS.)

1 TSP. OLIVE OIL

2 TSP. KOSHER SALT, DIVIDED

1/2 CUP WHITE RICE FLOUR

1/4 CUP SWEET RICE FLOUR (SOMETIMES LABELED MOCHIKO)

2 EGGS

1 TBSP. GRATED PARMESAN CHEESE

3 TBSP. TAPIOCA STARCH

1/4 TSP. GROUND NUTMEG

1/2 TSP. WHITE PEPPER

1. Preheat the oven to 350°F. Rinse the potatoes, poke them with a fork, rub them with olive oil, and sprinkle about 1 tsp. kosher salt on them. It's not an exact science. Bake until softened, about 1 hour. Cool the potatoes for 1 hour, then peel.

2. In a mixing bowl, combine the rice flours. Sprinkle a little of the flour mixture onto a large prep surface. Using a potato ricer or grater, rice or grate the peeled potatoes. Make a well in the middle of the pile of riced potatoes. Crack the eggs into the well, then sprinkle the cheese, tapioca starch, nutmeg, pepper, and remaining 1 tsp. salt around the ring of potatoes. With your fingertips, beat the eggs, then slowly mix them into the potatoes in a circular motion. Add most of the rice flour as you mix everything together, again using just your fingertips.

3. Once everything is well mixed, start kneading the dough until you have a nice-looking little loaf. Keep adding rice flour as you knead until it reaches a dough-like consistency. Divide the dough into 6 chunks, then roll each chunk into a thin rope. Cut the rope into bite-sized pieces. Sprinkle a little flour over everything if it starts to stick.

4. Before cooking all of the gnocchi, test a couple in boiling water—if they fall apart before floating, add more flour. To preserve them for later, place them on a baking sheet lined with parchment paper and freeze overnight; they can then be put in freezer bags and frozen for up to 6 months.

5. To cook the gnocchi, drop them in boiling, salted water, and fish them out when once they start floating. It should take only a couple minutes. Drain and toss with whatever you'd like—butter, Simple Basil Pesto (page 54), or Basic Red Sauce (page 53).

Sweet Potato Poi
(Poi 'Uala)

SERVES: 4

PREP TIME: 5 MINUTES

COOKING TIME: 1 HOUR

Poi is a Polynesian staple food that is typically made with mashed taro root; however, the Hawaiian people also traditionally made poi from sweet potato and breadfruit. Coconut milk adds sweetness and depth of flavor to this dish. Its creamy texture and sweet taste are perfect accompaniments to my Kalua Pig (page 180) and Lomi Lomi Salmon (page 234) recipes.

3 MEDIUM SWEET POTATOES (~1 1/2 LBS.), CUT IN HALF

1 (14 OZ.) CAN COCONUT MILK

1/2 TSP. SEA SALT

1. Place a steamer rack in a stockpot. Fill the pot with water until it starts to touch the bottom of the steamer rack, about 1½". Put the sweet potatoes on the steamer rack, cover with a lid, and steam on medium-high heat until soft to the touch, about 25 minutes. Check the water level about 15 minutes into steaming to make sure that the water hasn't evaporated; add more hot water if needed.

2. Turn off the heat, remove the sweet potatoes, and allow to cool for 15 minutes. Empty the stockpot and rinse clean. Warm the coconut milk in a separate pot on low while the potatoes cool. Once they are cool, slip the skins off the potatoes and discard, then put the peeled potatoes back in the stockpot.

3. Mash the potatoes with a potato masher or whisk, then add the salt and stir in the warm coconut milk, mixing until you get the right consistency—somewhere between mashed potatoes and pea soup. If you run out of coconut milk, add water until you get the desired consistency. For an extra-smooth poi, run the poi through a blender or use an immersion blender. Serve at room temperature. Leftovers will keep in the fridge for a week.

Parsnip Puree

Before the potato arrived in Europe, parsnips were one of the main staple crops throughout the region. First cultivated in Eurasia, parsnips were spread across Europe by the Romans. Due to their natural sweetness, parsnips were often served sweetened with honey or in fruitcakes for dessert.

Parsnip puree is just the start when it comes to puréed root vegetables. Turnips, carrots, sweet potatoes, celery root, and rutabaga can all be puréed (alone or in combinations) to delicious effect using the method below.

SERVES: 6
PREP TIME: 10 MINUTES
COOKING TIME: 50 MINUTES

2 LBS. PARSNIPS, CUT INTO LARGE CHUNKS

4 CLOVES GARLIC

10 BLACK PEPPERCORNS

2 BAY LEAVES

6 TBSP. BUTTER, CUBED

1/2 TSP. GROUND NUTMEG

1 TSP. SEA SALT

1. Place the parsnips in a large pot. Wrap the garlic, peppercorns, and bay leaves in cheesecloth and tie together, then add to the pot. Fill the pot with water until the parsnips are covered by 1". Bring to a boil, reduce the heat, and simmer until easily pierced with a fork, about 40 minutes.

2. Drain the parsnips and discard the cheesecloth. Purée the parsnips, in batches if needed, with a food processor or an immersion blender. Stir in the butter, nutmeg, and salt, and whip with a potato masher or whisk until smooth. Add more salt and butter to taste.

Tostones

Tostones are twice-fried plantains. The dish is common in many Central and South American countries, although it is sometimes known by other names.

Plantains and bananas are different varieties from the same parent plant. The banana plant originated in the eastern Indonesian islands as many as 9,000 years ago, where it spread throughout Asia before making its way to Africa. Portuguese sailors brought banana plants from West Africa to the Americas in the 16th century, and bananas and plantains have been an important part of Central and South American cuisine ever since.

SERVES: 4
PREP TIME: 5 MINUTES
COOKING TIME: 25 MINUTES

3-4 MOSTLY GREEN PLANTAINS (A FEW RIPE SPOTS ARE OKAY)

1/4 CUP COCONUT OIL

SALT TO TASTE

1. Peel and slice the plantains into 1" slices, slicing along the peel with a sharp knife to make peeling easier. Heat the oil in a skillet on medium-low heat until hot, about 3 minutes. Add the plantains and partially fry, turning every 30-60 seconds, about 3 minutes per piece. They will turn bright yellow as they fry; be careful not to brown them. Drain on paper towels as you fry them in batches, and let cool.

2. Smash the plantains to about ½" thickness. A tostonera is a smashing device made of 2 boards joined by a hinge, with a divot for the plantain; while a tostonera makes the job easy, you can also smash the plantains between 2 paper bags using the bottom of a plate.

3. Once your plantains are smashed, re-fry them. Reheat the oil on medium heat until hot, then add the smashed plantains. Fry on each side until golden brown, about 2 minutes per side. Drain on paper towels, sprinkle with salt to taste, and serve.

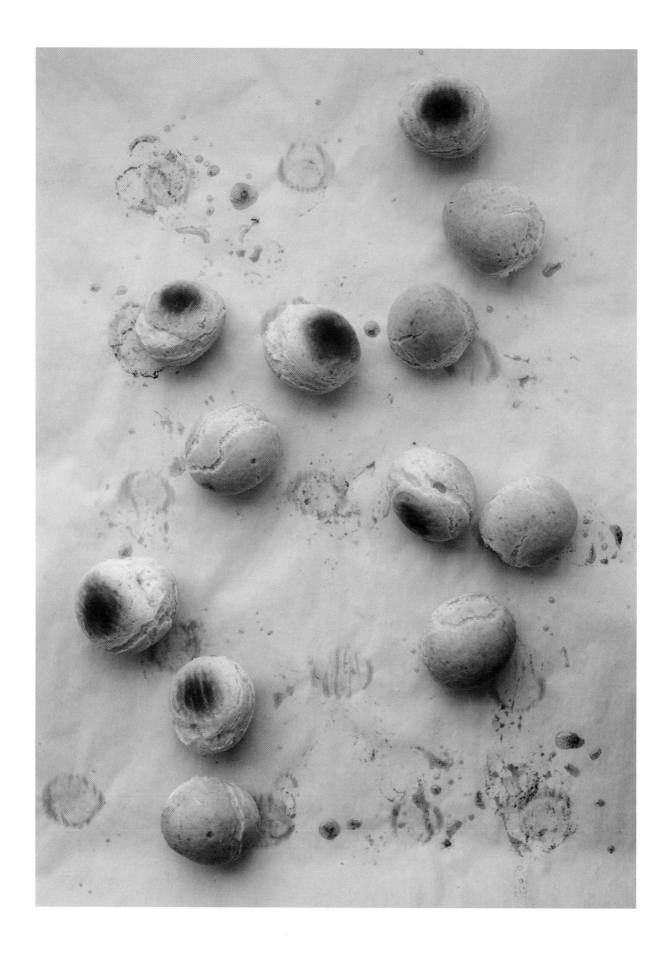

Pão de Queijo
(Brazilian Cheese Buns)

Pão de queijo is a traditional cheese bun popular in South America, especially in Brazil. The dish has been around since the 17th century and was made with just tapioca starch and water before the widespread domestication of cattle in Brazil during the 19th century led to the addition of cheese. Today, it's a popular breakfast food and can be found in most bakeries in Brazil.

Tapioca starch is often labeled as tapioca flour, cassava starch, or yuca starch; they are all the same thing.

SERVES: 6

PREP TIME: 10 MINUTES

COOKING TIME: 20 MINUTES

1 1/2 CUPS TAPIOCA STARCH

1/4 CUP HEAVY CREAM

1/4 CUP WATER

1 TBSP. BUTTER

1/2 TSP. SEA SALT

1 EGG, BEATEN

1/2 CUP GRATED HARD CHEESE (SUCH AS PARMESAN OR SHARP CHEDDAR)

1. Put the tapioca starch in a large mixing bowl and set aside. In a saucepan, combine the cream, water, butter, and salt and warm on medium-low heat. Once the butter melts and the liquid just starts to bubble, remove from the heat and stir it into the tapioca starch. Let the mixture cool for 5 minutes. Preheat the oven to 400°F.

2. Add the beaten egg to the mixture and knead with your hands. Add the cheese and mix together until it's dough-like. Add more starch and cheese if needed.

3. Roll the dough into 1" balls; you should be able to make 15-20 balls. Place the balls on a baking sheet and bake until golden brown, 15-20 minutes. You can also freeze the balls prior to baking to have a premade snack that can be ready after 20-25 minutes of baking.

4. To make breadsticks, form the dough into breadstick shapes before baking (see the picture on page 95).

Pizza

Pizza can be traced back to ancient Greece, where they covered bread with oil and cheese and reheated it. Italy is credited for adding tomatoes to pizza following their introduction from the New World in the 16th century. Surprisingly, the combination of tomatoes and cheese wasn't popular for hundreds of years, mostly until the famous Pizza Margherita incident captured on the cover of this book. The combination of tomatoes, mozzarella cheese, and basil leaves was served to Queen Margherita in 1889 to represent the Italian flag.

Pizzerias existed in the United States at the turn of the 20th century, but they were frequented mostly by Italian immigrants. Soldiers returning from the European campaign of World War II raved about pizza, and it became the sensation it is now almost overnight.

SERVES: 3-4 (MAKES 2 PIZZAS)

PREP TIME: 10 MINUTES

COOKING TIME: 40 MINUTES (FOR 2 PIZZAS)

1 1/2 CUPS TAPIOCA STARCH

1/4 CUP HEAVY CREAM

1/4 CUP WATER

2 TBSP. BUTTER

1/2 TSP. SEA SALT

1 EGG, BEATEN

3/4 CUP GRATED PARMESAN CHEESE (OR ANY HARD CHEESE)

PINCH OF WHITE PEPPER

1/4 TSP. DRIED OREGANO

1/2 CUP PIZZA SAUCE (BLENDED BASIC RED SAUCE, PAGE 53), DIVIDED

2/3 CUP GRATED MOZZARELLA, DIVIDED

TOPPINGS AS DESIRED

1. Put the tapioca starch in a large mixing bowl and set aside. In a saucepan, combine the cream, water, butter, and salt and warm on medium-low heat. Once the butter melts and the liquid just starts to bubble, remove from the heat and stir it into the tapioca starch. Let the mixture cool for 5 minutes. Preheat the oven to 500°F.

2. Add the beaten egg to the mixture and knead together with your hands. Add the Parmesan cheese, white pepper, and oregano and mix together until it's dough-like. Add more starch and cheese if needed. Depending on the ambient temperature of your kitchen, the starch can sometimes melt into a gooey consistency—if this happens, add more cheese until it's doughy enough to form into a pizza, and it'll turn out fine.

3. Split the dough in half, then stretch out each half into the thinnest disc possible without tearing. Put one half of the dough in a 8"-10" cast-iron skillet, spreading to the edges of the skillet with your fingers. Try to get it as thin as possible. With a fork, poke some holes in the dough to let air pass through.

4. Bake in the center of the oven for 6 minutes, then take it out and put it on the stovetop. Add half of the pizza sauce, mozzarella, and toppings—whatever you like. This step is important because it gives the dough time to cook through without burning the toppings.

5. Put the pizza back in the oven and bake for another 8-10 minutes or until the cheese starts to brown. For extra-crispy toppings, broil for the last minute or two of cooking.

6. Repeat the process with the other half of the dough.

7. This pizza also cooks well on a pizza stone. For best results, bake the crust for 8 minutes instead of 6 during the first stage of cooking.

CHAPTER 5
RED MEATS

Hearty Stew

Stew is a catchall term for solid ingredients cooked in liquid. It is one of the most ancient forms of cooking, and it's no surprise that the concept is often associated with comfort foods. After all, stews are irreversibly linked to human survival; they make raw foods edible and tough meats tender. As Paul mentioned in the Foreword, the first cooking tools used to make stews were likely animal hides. Turtle and mollusk shells were also used as ancient cookware.

This stew recipe has no direct point of origin, although it is not dissimilar to many European stews, like the French pot-au-feu. It can be made with beef, lamb, or bison.

SERVES: 4

PREP TIME: 20 MINUTES

COOKING TIME: 2 1/2 HOURS

2 LBS. STEW MEAT, CHUCK ROAST, OR SIMILAR, CUT INTO 1 1/2" CHUNKS

1/2 TSP. SEA SALT

1/2 TSP. BLACK PEPPER

1 TBSP. COCONUT OIL

1 MEDIUM ONION, FINELY CHOPPED

2 CLOVES GARLIC, MINCED

1/4 CUP RED WINE

1 CUP BEEF STOCK OR BROTH (PAGE 42)

1 CUP CHICKEN STOCK OR BROTH (PAGE 42)

1/2 TSP. DRIED THYME

2 BAY LEAVES

2 LARGE RUSSET POTATOES, PEELED AND CUT INTO BITE-SIZED CHUNKS

2 CARROTS, CUT INTO BITE-SIZED CHUNKS

1 PARSNIP, CUT INTO BITE-SIZED CHUNKS

1/2 CUP FROZEN PEAS

1 SMALL HANDFUL FRESH PARSLEY, CHOPPED

1. Season the meat with the salt and pepper. In a Dutch oven, heat the oil on medium until shimmering, about 2 minutes. Add the meat and brown, in batches if needed, turning every few minutes. Set the browned meat aside.

2. Preheat the oven to 300°F. Add the onion to the Dutch oven and sauté until softened, about 5 minutes. Add the garlic and sauté for another 30 seconds, then add the beef and its accumulated juices, wine, broths, thyme, and bay leaves. Add more broth if needed to mostly cover the beef. Bring to a simmer, cover, and put in the oven to roast for 1 hour 15 minutes.

3. Add the potatoes, carrots, and parsnip to the Dutch oven. Roast for another 40 minutes, until the vegetables and meat are tender. Remove from the oven, uncover, and place on the stovetop to simmer on low heat as you prepare the vegetable puree below; discard the bay leaves.

4. Using a ladle or large spoon, remove some of the potatoes, carrots, and parsnips, about 1 cup total, and ½ cup of the broth. Blend the vegetables and broth into a smooth puree, then return it to the Dutch oven, stirring until thick, about 1 minute. Carefully stir in the peas, then cover and simmer for 5 minutes. Season with salt and pepper to taste, garnish with fresh parsley, and serve.

Eye of Round Roast

Eye of round is cut from a section of the cow's hindquarters. It is a very lean and tough cut of meat due to the fact that it gets a lot of use. While braising is the most popular method of tenderizing lean meats, roasting at high heat can also produce a tender, flavorful dinner. This is my family's go-to roasting technique, as it allows us to transform a cheap cut of beef into a succulent roast in a relatively short time.

This recipe can be used with similar lean boneless roasts, like bottom round or rump roast. Adding root vegetables to the skillet or baking sheet adds another tasty dimension to your meal.

SERVES: 6-8

PREP TIME: 45 MINUTES

COOKING TIME: 1-2 HOURS

1 TSP. KOSHER SALT

1 TSP. COARSE-GROUND BLACK PEPPER

6 CLOVES GARLIC, MINCED

1/2 TSP. DRIED THYME

3-4 LBS. EYE OF ROUND ROAST (OR SIMILAR LEAN BONELESS ROAST)

1 TBSP. RED WINE

2 TBSP. WATER

1. Combine the salt, pepper, garlic, and thyme in a small bowl. Pat the roast dry with paper towels; rub the seasoning mixture all over the roast, then let it sit out for 30 minutes at room temperature. Preheat the oven to 500°F.

2. Place the roast on a baking sheet or stainless-steel skillet, fatty side up, and roast for 7 minutes per pound. Reduce the heat to 180°F and roast until the internal temperature reaches 135-140°F, about 1 hour. This process will create a roast that is dark brown and crusty on the outside and pink in the middle. Start checking the roast's internal temperature with a quick-read thermometer at the 30-minute mark, and every 15 minutes after that. Use these temperatures to gauge the roast's doneness (for best results, aim for medium-rare to medium-well):

- 125°F = rare
- 130°F = medium-rare
- 135°F = medium
- 150°F = medium-well
- 160°F = well-done

Remove the roast and set on a cutting board to rest for 5 minutes, then carve into thin slices.

3. If you used a stainless-steel skillet, place the skillet and the roast drippings on the stovetop; otherwise, transfer the drippings to a saucepan. Heat the pan on medium for 1 minute, then add the red wine and water, deglazing the pan and whisking to break up any chunks. Deglaze for 2 minutes, then strain through a fine mesh strainer and pour over the sliced roast.

Leftovers are best eaten cold, as reheating toughens the meat.

Shepherd's Pie

Although meat pies have been eaten in the British Isles since the Middle Ages, shepherd's pie as we know it today coincided with the arrival of the potato in Europe in the 16th century—although potatoes didn't catch on in Great Britain until the 18th century. Shepherd's pie appeared shortly thereafter, though under its original name, cottage pie, and made mostly with beef. The name shepherd's pie followed about 100 years later, along with the idea that it should be made with mutton. Today, shepherd's pie can be made with beef or lamb, or sometimes both, while cottage pie usually refers only to the beef version of the dish.

Another interesting fact about this dish is that it's prevalent in many other cultures with some pretty amusing names, like French Canada's pâté chinois *("Chinese pie"), Russia's* картофельная запеканка *("potato baked pudding"), and Brazil's* escondidinho *("hidden").*

SERVES: 6
PREP TIME: 20 MINUTES
COOKING TIME: 1 HOUR

2 LBS. RUSSET OR YUKON GOLD POTATOES, PEELED AND CUT INTO 1" CHUNKS

3 TBSP. BUTTER, DIVIDED

~1/2 CUP HEAVY CREAM

1 1/2 TSP. SEA SALT, DIVIDED

2 TSP. BLACK PEPPER, DIVIDED

1 1/2 LBS. GROUND BEEF, GROUND LAMB, OR A MIXTURE

1 SMALL ONION, FINELY CHOPPED

1 MEDIUM CARROT, DICED

1 CELERY ROOT, PEELED AND DICED

1 TBSP. TOMATO PASTE

2 CLOVES GARLIC, MINCED

1/2 CUP CHICKEN BROTH (PAGE 42)

1 TSP. WORCESTERSHIRE SAUCE

1 SMALL HANDFUL FRESH THYME, MINCED (ABOUT 1 TSP.)

1 SMALL HANDFUL FRESH ROSEMARY, MINCED (ABOUT 1 TSP.)

1/2 CUP FROZEN PEAS

1. Place the potatoes in a large stockpot and fill with enough water to cover the potatoes by 1". Bring to a boil, reduce the heat to medium, and simmer until fork-tender, about 15 minutes. Drain well, then return to the pot and add 2 Tbsp. of the butter. Mash until smooth and firm, adding cream as needed, up to ½ cup. Season with salt and pepper to taste (about 1 tsp. each), then set aside.

2. In a cast-iron skillet, brown the ground meat on medium heat until most of the pink is cooked out, about 6 minutes. Drain and set aside the rendered fat, then set aside the cooked meat. Return 2 Tbsp. of the rendered fat to the pan, as well as the remaining 1 Tbsp. butter, and warm it on medium heat until melted. Add the onion, carrot, and celery root and sauté until softened, about 8 minutes.

3. Add the tomato paste and garlic and sauté for another 2 minutes. Add the chicken broth, Worcestershire sauce, herbs, and more salt and pepper to taste (about ½ tsp. salt and 1 tsp. pepper). Simmer until slightly thickened, about 3 minutes. Remove from the heat and stir in the ground meat and frozen peas.

4. Preheat the oven to 450°F. Spread the meat mixture evenly in the skillet, then top the meat mixture with globs of mashed potatoes. Spread with a spatula or fork. Bake until the potatoes are browned, about 30 minutes. Let rest for 5 minutes before serving.

Salisbury Steak

Salisbury steak was developed in the late 19th century by Dr. J. H. Salisbury to help maintain ideal health if eaten exclusively. (He believed that the overconsumption of starches, fruits, and vegetables was to blame for most ailments.) While his reasoning doesn't quite hold up to the test of time, his dish has endured. It rose to fame in the 1960s and 1970s and became synonymous with TV dinners in the United States.

While a strict mincemeat regimen is probably far from ideal in terms of both taste and health, Salisbury steak makes for a hearty, comforting meal. Similar dishes are popular worldwide, especially in Japan (hanbagu steak) and Russia (котлета).

SERVES: 2
PREP TIME: 10 MINUTES
COOKING TIME: 20 MINUTES

---

1 LB. GROUND BEEF

1 EGG

2 TBSP. ALMOND MEAL

1/2 TSP. SEA SALT

1/2 TSP. GROUND MUSTARD

1/2 TSP. ONION POWDER

1/4 TSP. BAKING SODA

1/4 TSP. CREAM OF TARTAR

1 TSP. BLACK PEPPER, DIVIDED

2 CUPS BEEF BROTH (PAGE 42)

5 OZ. (1/2 PKG.) SLICED WHITE MUSHROOMS

1 TBSP. HEAVY CREAM

2 TSP. ARROWROOT STARCH

2 TSP. COLD WATER

1. Preheat the oven to 350°F. Combine the ground beef, egg, almond meal, salt, mustard, onion powder, baking soda, cream of tartar, and ½ tsp. of the pepper in a mixing bowl. Mix with your hands until everything is well combined; be careful not to overmix.

2. Form the meat into 4 steak-shaped patties and place on a baking sheet. Bake until browned, about 18 minutes, then broil for 2 minutes to create a crust.

3. While the steaks are cooking, combine the broth, mushrooms, and the remaining ½ tsp. pepper in a small saucepan. Bring to a simmer on medium heat, then reduce the heat to medium-low and simmer until the mushrooms shrink and soften, about 15 minutes. Stir in the cream and reduce the heat to low. In a separate dish, mix together the starch and cold water to create a slurry. Stir the starch slurry into the broth and simmer until thickened, about 3 minutes. Add salt and pepper to taste, then plate the steaks and pour the gravy on top.

Chicken-Fried Steak

Also known as country-fried steak, chicken-fried steak is a staple of Southern cuisine in the United States. It gained its name from the fact that it is prepared like Southern Fried Chicken (page 194). It is commonly believed that chicken-fried steak was created by German and Austrian immigrants in Texas in the 1800s.

Chicken-fried steak is a great meal for those on a budget, as cube steak (sometimes called minute steak) is generally easy to find and very cheap. If cube steak is unavailable in your area, you can make your own using bottom round and a blade meat tenderizer.

SERVES: 6

PREP TIME: 25 MINUTES

COOKING TIME: 45 MINUTES

1/2 CUP WHITE RICE FLOUR

1 TSP. SEA SALT

1/2 TSP. PAPRIKA

1/2 TSP. GARLIC POWDER

2 TSP. COARSE-GROUND BLACK PEPPER, DIVIDED

4 EGGS, BEATEN (OR 2 EGGS MIXED WITH 1/4 CUP HEAVY CREAM)

1/2 CUP POTATO STARCH

1/2 CUP TAPIOCA STARCH

2 LBS. CUBE STEAK

1/4 CUP LARD OR COCONUT OIL

3 TBSP. BUTTER

2 CUPS BEEF BROTH (PAGE 42)

1/2 TSP. FRESH THYME (DRIED IS OKAY)

2 TBSP. HEAVY CREAM

1. In a large pan or shallow bowl, combine the rice flour, salt, paprika, garlic powder, and 1 tsp. of the pepper. In a like-sized pan or bowl, place the beaten eggs. In a third like-sized pan or bowl, combine the other half of the pepper with the starches. Gently pound the cube steak to an even thickness, about ¼"; slice into pieces the size of large steaks. Dredge the steaks in the rice flour mixture, then the eggs, then the starch mixture, shaking off the excess as you go. Place the steaks on a wire rack and let rest for 10 minutes. Reserve 3 Tbsp. of the rice flour mixture.

2. Preheat the oven to 170°F. Heat the lard or coconut oil in a cast-iron skillet on medium heat for 5 minutes. Add the steaks and fry in batches until golden brown, about 5 minutes per side. Place the cooked steaks on a different wire rack supported by a baking sheet, then place in the oven to keep warm while you cook the others. Add more lard or coconut oil as needed while frying.

3. Remove everything but the browned bits at the bottom of the skillet. Reduce the heat to medium-low and melt the butter in the skillet. Stir in the reserved rice flour mixture and toast until aromatic, about 2 minutes. Stir in the beef broth and thyme and continue to stir as it thickens, about 2 minutes. Gently scrape up any browned pieces into the gravy. Once it has thickened, stir in the cream and remove from the heat. Season with salt and pepper to taste and serve the gravy over the steaks.

Chili Con Carne

Chili con carne, more commonly known simply as chili, is a type of stew originally created by American frontier settlers. The original dish known as chili was prepared by Aztec and Mayan chefs and consisted of beans served in a tomato sauce seasoned with chile peppers. Settlers in the 1800s added pieces of dried beef to the dish, and chili con carne was born. By the early 1900s, chili parlors had sprouted up in Texas and beyond.

To me, chili is best when it is versatile and evenly flavored. Adding chocolate and mayonnaise sound counterintuitive at first, but they give the dish a rich, smooth taste. This chili is relatively free of large chunks and goes well served over other foods, including rice, French fries, hot dogs, and hamburgers.

SERVES: 6
PREP TIME: 5 MINUTES
COOKING TIME: 2 1/2 HOURS

1 TBSP. BUTTER

1 MEDIUM ONION, COARSELY CHOPPED

6 CLOVES GARLIC, MINCED

1 1/2 TBSP. GROUND CORIANDER

1 TBSP. GROUND CUMIN

1 TSP. SEA SALT

1 TSP. BLACK PEPPER

1 TSP. PAPRIKA

1 TSP. OREGANO

1 TSP. CAYENNE PEPPER

1 TSP. RED PEPPER FLAKES

2 BAY LEAVES

2 LBS. GROUND BEEF OR GAME MEAT (SUCH AS VENISON OR ELK)

1 (14.5 OZ.) CAN DICED TOMATOES

2 (14.5 OZ.) CANS PURÉED TOMATOES

8 OZ. SMOKED SAUSAGE (LINGUIÇA OR ANDOUILLE PREFERRED), CUT IN HALF LENGTHWISE AND SLICED INTO HALF-MOONS

2 TBSP. MAYONNAISE (PAGE 50)

2 TBSP. UNSWEETENED COCOA POWDER

GRATED CHEDDAR CHEESE AND SOUR CREAM FOR SERVING (OPTIONAL)

1. In a stockpot, warm the butter on medium heat for 1 minute, then add the onion and sauté until aromatic, about 5 minutes. Add the garlic, spices, and bay leaves and sauté for another minute. Add the ground beef and simmer until browned, stirring frequently to break up chunks, about 6 minutes. Add the tomatoes, cover, and reduce the heat to low; simmer for 1 hour.

2. Near the end of the hour, brown the sausage slices in a separate pan on medium heat, about 3 minutes per side.

3. After 1 hour, add the browned sausage to the chili. Simmer, uncovered, for another hour. Stir in the mayonnaise and cocoa powder and simmer for another 10 minutes to allow the flavors to marry; add more salt, pepper, and cayenne pepper (or hot sauce) to taste. Top with cheddar cheese and sour cream if desired.

Barbecue Brisket

Brisket, the tough pectoral muscle of the cow, requires an extended cooking time. It is commonly used for slow cooking, as seen with corned beef and pot roasts. A whole brisket is often butchered into two pieces, the flat and the point. The flat cut is very lean and almost pure muscle, while the fattier point cut rests on top of the flat, with a layer of fat between them. Cooking with either the point cut or a whole brisket is preferred but not necessary. This recipe works with a whole brisket or either cut—the cooking time is the only element that changes.

SERVES: 10
PREP TIME: UP TO 1 HOUR
COOKING TIME: UP TO 4 HOURS

6-8 LBS. BRISKET, EXCESS FAT TRIMMED TO 1/4" THICKNESS

1/3 CUP ALL-PURPOSE BEEF RUB (PAGE 47)

HICKORY OR PECAN WOOD CHUNKS, OR A COMBINATION

1/2 CUP BEEF BROTH (PAGE 42)

2 TSP. ONION POWDER

2 TSP. GARLIC POWDER

2 TSP. BLACK PEPPER

2 TBSP. BARBECUE SAUCE (PAGE 48)

1. Rub the brisket with the beef rub, wrap in plastic wrap, and refrigerate for at least 30 minutes or up to 1 hour. Remove and discard the plastic wrap.

2. Prepare your grill for indirect smoking with hickory as your smoking wood (see page 36). Bring the smoker temperature to 300°F, then smoke the brisket, fatty side down and thick side facing the heat, at 275-325°F until it reaches an internal temperature of 165°F, about 2 hours. Wrap in heavy-duty aluminum foil with the beef broth, onion powder, garlic powder, and pepper. Return the brisket to the smoker and continue to cook until a toothpick can penetrate the meat without resistance and the internal temperature reaches 200-205°F, about 1 additional hour.

3. Remove the meat from the aluminum foil and place directly on the grill, reserving the liquid. Brush a thin layer of barbecue sauce on each side and allow it to caramelize under direct high heat, about 2 minutes per side. Let rest for 15 minutes before slicing against the grain.

4. As the brisket rests, separate the fat from the reserved braising liquid using a fat separator and serve the defatted liquid alongside the brisket, mixing with additional barbecue sauce if desired.

Stuffed Cabbage Rolls

Cabbage rolls are found all over Europe, Asia, and the Middle East. They are staple dishes in Croatia, Poland, the Ukraine, Russia, and Sweden; this recipe follows the Russian interpretation.

There is some controversy over the origin of the dish. One common theory is based on its name, which could be linked to the Russian word for pigeons (goluby), which is very close to the word for cabbage rolls (golubsy). Russian cuisine and culture were heavily influenced by the French in the 17th and 18th centuries, and these stuffed cabbage rolls could be an attempt to re-create roasted pigeons, a popular French dish at the time.

SERVES: 6
PREP TIME: 10 MINUTES
COOKING TIME: 2 HOURS

6 TBSP. BUTTER, DIVIDED

1 ONION, FINELY CHOPPED

6 CLOVES GARLIC, MINCED

1 LB. GROUND BEEF

1 TSP. SEA SALT

1 1/2 TSP. BLACK PEPPER, DIVIDED

1 TSP. DRIED DILL

1 TSP. MUSTARD POWDER

2 CUPS WARM COOKED RICE (PAGE 96)

2 CARROTS, SHREDDED (~1/2 CUP)

1 HEAD GREEN CABBAGE

1 (14 OZ.) CAN TOMATO SAUCE

1. Warm 2 Tbsp. of the butter over medium heat, then add the onion and sauté until softened, about 6 minutes. Add the garlic and sauté for another minute, then add the ground beef, salt, 1 tsp. of the pepper, dill, and mustard powder. Continue to cook, stirring frequently, until most of the pink has been cooked out of the beef, about 6 minutes. Stir in the cooked rice and carrots, then remove from the heat and set aside as you prepare the cabbage.

2. Cut out the core of the cabbage. Bring a stockpot of water to a boil on high heat. Drop the cabbage into the boiling water and press it down with a wooden spoon, boiling for 5 minutes. Carefully remove the cabbage from the water using 2 forks and strain in a colander for 1 minute, but keep the water boiling. Peel off the softened cabbage leaves, stopping when the leaves get hard and dry. Return the head of cabbage to the water, repeating the process.

3. Heat the remaining 4 Tbsp. butter in a saucepan on low. Stir in the tomato sauce and the remaining ½ tsp. pepper; allow to simmer while you make the rolls. Place the softened cabbage leaves on a cutting board and shave off the excess spine from the outer side of each leaf. Spoon some filling into the base end of the cabbage leaf and roll it together, tucking in the sides as you roll. One head of cabbage should yield 15-18 rolls.

4. Preheat the oven to 325°F. Place the rolls in a casserole dish, then spoon the tomato sauce over the rolls. Bake until cooked through, about 40 minutes.

Borscht

Borscht (Борщ) is a hearty soup most commonly associated with Russia, Poland, and the Ukraine. Its name likely comes from the Slavic name for hogweed (Borschevik), which was often used to flavor soups. Although potatoes were a later addition, the foundation of borscht as we know it today dates back at least to the 9th century. This recipe is the popular Russian version, which is served hot and with meat. To cut down on the cooking time, you could make this soup with premade broth, or even make it vegetarian by using just water. Instructions for each variation are provided below.

SERVES: 8

PREP TIME: 30 MINUTES

COOKING TIME: 3 HOURS

---

2 CARROTS, DIVIDED

1 ONION, DIVIDED

3 LBS. BEEF BONES WITH MEAT ATTACHED (OXTAILS, SHANKS, KNUCKLES, OR A COMBINATION)

1 TSP. BLACK PEPPERCORNS

2 LARGE BEETS

1/2 TBSP. OLIVE OIL

3 TBSP. BUTTER

1 CLOVE GARLIC, MINCED

2 TBSP. TOMATO PASTE

1/4 CUP RED WINE VINEGAR

1/2 HEAD GREEN CABBAGE, SHREDDED

2 RUSSET OR YUKON GOLD POTATOES, PEELED AND CUBED

2 BAY LEAVES

1 SMALL HANDFUL PARSLEY, COARSELY CHOPPED

JUICE OF 1/2 LEMON (1 TBSP.)

SALT AND BLACK PEPPER TO TASTE

SOUR CREAM AND FRESH DILL FOR SERVING

1. Over an open flame or under a broiler, roast 1 carrot and half of the onion until charred, about 3 minutes. Boil the bones in a large stockpot filled with water for 8 minutes, then drain and rinse thoroughly with cold water. Clean the stockpot, then return the bones to the pot along with the charred carrot and half onion and the peppercorns. Add enough cold water to cover the bones by at least 1", about 4 quarts. Bring to a boil, then reduce the heat and simmer on medium-low until the meat easily separates from the bone, about 2 hours. Be sure to skim any foam or fat that accumulates on the surface. Add water to replace any that evaporates.

2. As the bones simmer, preheat the oven to 375°F. Place the beets in aluminum foil, drizzle with the olive oil, and wrap tightly. Roast until easily pierced with a fork, 45-60 minutes. Remove from the oven, let cool, then slip off the skins and cut the beets into French fry–sized strips. Set aside.

3. When the bones are ready, strain the broth and discard the vegetables and peppercorns, then return the broth to the stockpot. Set the meaty bones aside to cool; once cool, pick apart the meat and set aside. Discard the bones or reserve for making stock.

4. Coarsely chop the remaining half onion and grate the other carrot. In a skillet, warm the butter on medium heat, then add the chopped onion and sauté until softened, about 5 minutes. Add the minced garlic and tomato paste and sauté until aromatic, about 1 minute. Add the sautéed onion and garlic paste to the broth, along with the beets, red wine vinegar, and grated carrot. Bring to a simmer on medium heat, then add the shredded cabbage and cubed potatoes. Return to a simmer and cook for 10 more minutes, skimming any excess fat from the surface, then stir in the meat, parsley, and lemon juice. Season with salt and pepper to taste, about ½ tsp. each.

5. Cover, remove from the heat, and allow to brew for 20 minutes. Serve with a dollop of sour cream and fresh dill sprinkled on top. For a more flavorful soup, allow the soup to brew overnight and reheat the next day.

6. To make this soup with premade broth, bring 2 quarts each water and beef broth to a simmer and proceed directly to step 2. To make it vegetarian, do the same but with 4 quarts water. Vegetarian borscht is often served cold.

Swedish Meatballs
(Köttbullar)

While meatballs have been around at least since the Middle Ages, they weren't documented in Sweden until the 18th century. Meatballs were likely an uncommon food in northern Europe until the widespread use of meat grinders; they later became standard smorgasbord (the original buffet!) fare. Scandinavian immigrants brought their meatballs to the United States, particularly the Midwest, in the 1920s.

SERVES: 4

PREP TIME: 15 MINUTES

COOKING TIME: 30 MINUTES

3 TBSP. BUTTER, DIVIDED

1/2 ONION, MINCED OR BLENDED IN A FOOD PROCESSOR

1/2 LB. GROUND BEEF

1/2 LB. GROUND PORK

1/4 TSP. SEA SALT

1/2 CUP HEAVY CREAM, DIVIDED

1/4 CUP ALMOND MEAL

1 EGG YOLK

1/4 TSP. GROUND NUTMEG

1/4 TSP. ALLSPICE

1/4 TSP. BAKING SODA

1/4 TSP. CREAM OF TARTAR

1/4 TSP. BLACK PEPPER

2 TBSP. WHITE RICE FLOUR

1/2 CUP BEEF BROTH, OR MORE IF NEEDED (PAGE 42)

1/2 TBSP. HONEY

1 BAY LEAF

FRESH DILL AND TART BERRIES FOR SERVING

1. In a large skillet, melt 1 Tbsp. of the butter on medium heat, then add the blended onion and sweat for 2 minutes. Scoop the onion into a mixing bowl, spreading it around to speed up the cooling process. Allow to cool, about 5 minutes. Add the ground meats, salt, ¼ cup of the cream, almond meal, egg yolk, nutmeg, allspice, baking soda, cream of tartar, and pepper. Mix thoroughly with your hands, then roll into 1" balls.

2. Return the skillet to the stovetop and warm another 1 Tbsp. butter on medium heat. Add some of the meatballs and sauté in batches until cooked through, about 8-10 minutes per batch, turning every few minutes with tongs. As the first batch is cooking, preheat the oven to 170°F. As each batch finishes cooking, put the meatballs in a large oven-safe dish and place in the oven to keep warm. Add more butter to the skillet for each batch if needed.

3. To make the gravy, melt the remaining 1 Tbsp. butter in the skillet on medium heat; add the white rice flour and toast until it starts to turn golden brown, about 2 minutes. Stir in the beef broth, honey, and bay leaf, then simmer for 3 minutes, stirring often, scraping up any remaining pieces of meatball. Add more broth if the gravy gets too thick. Season with salt and pepper to taste, then remove from the heat and stir in the remaining ¼ cup cream. Add the meatballs to the skillet and coat with gravy before serving. This dish is best served with mashed potatoes, fresh dill, and tart berries (such as lingonberries or raspberries).

Kalbi
(Korean Short Ribs)

Kalbi (often spelled galbi) is a marinated, grilled short rib dish that is both tasty and easy to prepare. In South Korea, kalbi is also made with whole short ribs that are butterflied so they remain thin. This style is called wang kalbi ("king ribs"), and the resulting flap of meat attached to the large short rib bone provides for a unique presentation; many kalbi enthusiasts are convinced that this style of kalbi has a superior taste. I find them equally delicious.

SERVES: 4

PREP TIME: 30 MINUTES PLUS OVERNIGHT

COOKING TIME: 10 MINUTES

MARINADE:

1 ASIAN PEAR OR GOLDEN OR BOSC PEAR, GRATED (OR 1/2 CUP UNSWEETENED APPLESAUCE)

6 CLOVES GARLIC, MINCED

1/2" GINGER, PEELED AND GRATED (OR 1 TSP. GROUND GINGER)

1 CUP SODA WATER

1/2 CUP TAMARI

1/4 CUP HONEY

1/4 CUP SESAME OIL

2 TBSP. SESAME SEEDS

JUICE OF 1 LIME (2 TBSP.)

3 LBS. BEEF SHORT RIBS, CUT ACROSS THE BONE (OFTEN REFERRED TO AS FLANKEN, ENGLISH, OR L.A. CUT)

1. Combine all the marinade ingredients, then pour over the ribs in a resealable plastic bag. Mix thoroughly to coat all the pieces evenly. Marinate overnight.

2. The next day, grill the ribs over direct high heat until cooked through, about 3 minutes per side. Serve with rice, Kimchi (page 72), and leaves of lettuce or perilla (described in my Gamjatang recipe, page 182) to wrap around the meat.

3. Kalbi is often dipped in Kochujang Sauce (page 80) or gireumjang, which is made by combining 2 parts salt and 1 part black pepper and adding sesame oil until it becomes a thick, grainy sauce.

Japchae

SERVES: 3-4

PREP TIME: 1 HOUR (TO MARINATE THE BEEF)

COOKING TIME: 20 MINUTES

A common party dish in Korea today, japchae has its origins in the 17th century; fittingly, it was first served at a party for the reigning king. Originally made with just vegetables and mushrooms, sweet potato noodles (also called glass noodles) were introduced in the 20th century and are now an integral part of the dish.

2 TSP. TAMARI

2 TSP. SESAME OIL

1 TSP. RICE WINE

1/2 TSP. WHITE PEPPER

1/2 TSP. SEA SALT

2 CLOVES GARLIC, MINCED

1/2" GINGER, PEELED AND MINCED

1/2 LB. RIB-EYE OR SIRLOIN STEAK, SLICED INTO STRIPS

1 TBSP. CHICKEN BROTH (PAGE 42)

1 TSP. HONEY

1/2 BUNCH (4 OZ.) SPINACH

6 OZ. SWEET POTATO NOODLES (DANGMYEON), CUT INTO 6" LENGTHS

1 TBSP. COCONUT OIL

1 CARROT, JULIENNED

3 SHIITAKE MUSHROOMS, FRESH OR RECONSTITUTED DRY (SOAKED FOR 30 MINUTES IN WARM WATER)

4 GREEN ONIONS, CUT INTO 1" SLICES

1 TBSP. TOASTED SESAME SEEDS, DIVIDED

1. Mix the tamari, sesame oil, rice wine, white pepper, salt, garlic, and ginger, then combine half of the resulting sauce with the beef strips and marinate for 1 hour. Combine the other half of the sauce with the chicken broth and honey and set aside.

2. As the beef marinates, prep the other ingredients. In a stockpot, bring some water to a boil. Parboil the spinach for 30 seconds, then remove with tongs, rinse, and squeeze until mostly dry. In the same water, gently boil the sweet potato noodles for 5 minutes, then drain and rinse with cold water; they will start to harden, which is fine. Toss the noodles with a little sesame oil to prevent sticking, then set aside.

3. Warm the coconut oil in a wok on medium-high heat until shimmering, about 1 minute. Add the beef and stir-fry until cooked through, about 3 minutes, then remove the beef and set aside. Add the carrot to the wok and stir-fry until slightly softened, about 1 minute, then add the noodles, spinach, mushrooms, green onions, beef, sauce, and half of the sesame seeds. Stir-fry until the sauce cooks down, stirring frequently, 2-3 minutes. Season to taste, then sprinkle the remaining sesame seeds over the japchae and serve.

Japanese Beef Curry

Curry is a relatively new dish to Japan, and it has a rich and interesting history. In the 19th century, sailors in the Japanese Navy often suffered from beriberi, a disease caused by a lack of vitamin B1 (thiamine), mostly due to the fact that their diet consisted almost exclusively of white rice. To solve the problem, the Japanese Navy tried to introduce bread, but it didn't catch on. In the early 20th century, the Japanese Navy observed that the British Navy served curry to their sailors and decided to follow suit, adding a wheat flour roux to the curry to increase its vitamin B1 content. The resulting starchy, sticky curry was an instant hit in the Navy and spread to the rest of the country from there. Today, curry houses are among the most prominent restaurants in Japan, and curry is a common daily meal; current estimates show that the average Japanese person eats curry at least once a week.

Making a Japanese curry without wheat flour is a challenge, but a rice flour roux creates a similar texture. The greatest difficulty in creating an authentic-tasting Japanese curry comes in finding the right combination of spices. I prefer to use store-bought S&B Oriental Curry Powder, but I have provided a recipe on the following page if you'd like to tackle the spice mix yourself.

SERVES: 6

PREP TIME: 10 MINUTES

COOKING TIME: 2 HOURS

1 TBSP. COCONUT OIL

2 LBS. CHUCK ROAST, CUT INTO 1 1/2" PIECES

1/2 ONION, COARSELY CHOPPED

3 RUSSET POTATOES, PEELED AND CUT INTO 1 1/2" CHUNKS

3 CARROTS, CUT INTO LARGE CHUNKS

3 TBSP. BUTTER

3 1/2 TBSP. RICE FLOUR

4 TBSP. S&B ORIENTAL CURRY POWDER (OR SEE RECIPE ON OPPOSITE PAGE)

2 TBSP. HONEY

4 OZ. APPLESAUCE (OR 1 GRATED APPLE)

2 TSP. SEA SALT

1. In a stockpot, warm the coconut oil on medium heat until shimmering, about 2 minutes. Brown the chuck roast, in batches if needed, for 3 minutes per side, then set aside. Add the onion and sauté until softened, about 4 minutes. Return the beef to the stockpot and add enough water to cover the meat by 1", about 1 quart. Bring to a simmer, cover, reduce the heat to low, and gently simmer until the beef is tender, about 1½ hours.

2. Stir in the potatoes and carrots, adding more water if needed to cover everything, then increase the heat to medium-low and simmer, uncovered, until the potatoes start to soften around the edges, about 10 minutes.

3. While the potatoes and carrots are simmering, prepare your rice flour roux. In a small saucepan, melt the butter on medium-low heat for 1 minute, then stir in the rice flour. Toast until slightly golden, about 2 minutes, then remove from the heat and set aside.

4. Once the potatoes are ready, gently stir in the roux, curry powder, honey, applesauce, and salt, being careful not to break up the potatoes. Simmer until thickened, stirring occasionally. Add more salt and honey to taste and serve with rice. This curry is fairly spicy, but if you want to make it spicier, add cayenne pepper or Japanese pepper powder (*Shichimi Tōgarashi*) to taste.

S+B Curry Powder

JAPANESE CURRY POWDER

If S&B Oriental Curry Powder is not available in your area, or if you want to tackle making it on your own, here is my best approximation of the powder combination.

1 TBSP. TURMERIC

1 TBSP. FENUGREEK SEEDS

1 TBSP. GROUND CUMIN

1 TBSP. CORIANDER SEEDS

1/2 TBSP. GROUND CINNAMON

1/2 TBSP. GROUND GINGER

1 TSP. CAYENNE PEPPER

1 TSP. BLACK PEPPER

1 TSP. GROUND STAR ANISE

1/2 TSP. GROUND CLOVES

1/2 TSP. FENNEL

1/2 TSP. GROUND NUTMEG

1/2 TSP. ALLSPICE

1 GREEN CARDAMOM POD, SEEDS REMOVED AND POD DISCARDED

1 BAY LEAF, SMASHED (OR 1 TSP. CRUSHED BAY LEAVES)

1. Combine all the ingredients in a mortar and grind with a pestle until smooth.

Loco Moco

SERVES: 2

PREP TIME: 5 MINUTES, PLUS TIME TO PREP THE RICE

COOKING TIME: 20 MINUTES

Loco moco is a popular dish on the Hawaiian islands. It's the ultimate breakfast meal prior to a big workday, consisting of rice, a hamburger patty, fried eggs, and brown gravy. It takes a couple tries to get the timing right so that the rice, hamburgers, gravy, and eggs are all ready at the same time, but once you have the method down, it'll quickly become a breakfast staple.

1/2 LB. GROUND BEEF

1 TSP. COCONUT OIL

2 CUPS BEEF BROTH (PAGE 42)

1 TSP. BLACK PEPPER

2 TBSP. ARROWROOT STARCH OR POTATO STARCH

2 CUPS COOKED WHITE RICE (PAGE 96) OR CAULIFLOWER RICE (PAGE 78)

2 EGGS

1. Form the ground beef into 2 patties. Warm the coconut oil in a cast-iron skillet on medium-high heat until shimmering, about 1 minute. Add the patties and pan-fry until cooked through, 3 minutes per side. Set aside.

2. In a small saucepan, combine the broth and pepper, then bring to a simmer on medium-low heat. In a small bowl, combine the starch and a little water to create a slurry. Slowly pour it into the broth, stirring as it thickens.

3. Place a scoop of rice on each plate, then add a hamburger patty. Fry 2 eggs and place 1 egg on each patty, then cover with gravy.

Beef Rendang

Rendang is a dry curry that originated among the Minangkabau people of West Sumatra and later spread throughout Indonesia and Malaysia. Its age is unknown, but historians have traced its origin as far back as 500 years.

There are three recognized forms of rendang in Minangkabau culture, each depending on the cooking time: a pale, lightly cooked curry known as gulai; a browned but still liquid curry called kalio; and a rich, dry, dark brown dish called rendang, the version prepared in this recipe. In other countries, most notably Malaysia and the Netherlands, the rendang most often served is closer to kalio.

While its extended cooking time can be a test of patience, it's well worth the wait; the aroma and overwhelming richness of rendang are unforgettable.

SERVES: 4

PREP TIME: 30 MINUTES

COOKING TIME: 2-3 HOURS

SPICE PASTE:

1 RED BELL PEPPER, STEM AND SEEDS REMOVED, COARSELY CHOPPED

5 SHALLOTS, QUARTERED

4 CLOVES GARLIC

1" GALANGAL, PEELED AND COARSELY CHOPPED

1" GINGER, PEELED AND COARSELY CHOPPED

6 MACADAMIA NUTS (RAW PREFERRED)

1 BIRD'S EYE CHILE, SEEDS AND RIBS REMOVED

2 TSP. SEA SALT

1/2 TSP. GROUND CLOVES

1/2 TSP. GROUND NUTMEG

1 TBSP. COCONUT OIL

2 1/2 LBS. CHUCK, CUT INTO 1 1/2" CHUNKS

4 STALKS LEMONGRASS, CUT INTO 3" PIECES

1 (14 OZ.) CAN COCONUT MILK

1 CINNAMON STICK

7 KAFFIR LIME LEAVES (FRESH PREFERRED; DRIED AVAILABLE ONLINE)

1 BAY LEAF

1. Combine the spice paste ingredients in a blender and blend into a fine paste, adding a little water if it gets too thick to purée.

2. In a large, shallow skillet, warm the coconut oil on medium heat for 1 minute, then add the blended spice paste; simmer until aromatic, about 5 minutes. Add the remaining ingredients and carefully stir until well combined.

3. Reduce the heat to medium-low and simmer, stirring every 10-15 minutes to prevent scorching, until the liquid has evaporated, the beef fat is rendered, and oil appears on the surface. It should take 2-3 hours. Reduce the heat to low if the sauce simmers too rapidly and appears to be boiling rather than simmering. The curry should have a slightly dry and oily texture. Serve with basmati rice steamed in ¼ cup coconut milk and 1 tsp. turmeric (page 96).

Pho

Pho, often considered the national dish of Vietnam, is a rice noodle soup that uses a beef bone broth. It's hard to describe the basic yet complex taste that comes from this unique mix of broth, beef, spices, and herbs. The dish emerged from Hanoi in the early 20th century and was brought to the United States in the 1970s by refugees after the fall of Saigon. The inclusion of beef in the dish reflects its French influence; prior to French colonialism, cows in Vietnam were used mainly for labor and not as a food source.

This is a time-consuming recipe, but it's worth every moment spent on it. Some Asian markets sell tea bags pre-filled with the whole spices, which is very convenient.

SERVES: 6

PREP TIME: 10 MINUTES

COOKING TIME: 7 HOURS

---

4 WHOLE STAR ANISE

4 GREEN CARDAMOM PODS

1 BLACK CARDAMOM POD

2 CINNAMON STICKS

1 TSP. CORIANDER SEEDS

1/4 TSP. FENNEL SEEDS

1/4 TSP. WHOLE CLOVES

3 LBS. OXTAIL AND KNUCKLE BONES

1 LARGE ONION, PEELED

1" GINGER, PEELED

2 LBS. BEEF BRISKET OR EYE OF ROUND ROAST

1 PARSNIP

2 TBSP. FISH SAUCE

1 TBSP. SEA SALT

16 OZ. RICE NOODLES

1 LARGE HANDFUL FRESH CILANTRO, COARSELY CHOPPED

4 GREEN ONIONS, FINELY CHOPPED

1 ONION, THINLY SLICED

1 LARGE HANDFUL THAI BASIL LEAVES

2 LIMES, CUT INTO WEDGES

2 JALAPEÑO PEPPERS, SLICED INTO RINGS

Pho Spices

1. In a saucepan, toast the spices on medium-low heat for about 5 minutes. Over an open flame or under a broiler, roast the onion and ginger until charred, about 3 minutes. Set aside.

2. Boil the oxtail and knuckle bones in a large stockpot filled with water for 8 minutes, then drain and rinse thoroughly with cold water. Clean the stockpot, then return the bones to the pot. Add enough cold water to cover the bones by at least 1", about 4 quarts. Bring to a boil on high heat, then reduce the heat to medium-low. Add the toasted spices, onion, ginger, brisket, parsnip, fish sauce, and salt. Simmer for 1½ hours, then remove the brisket with tongs and submerge in a bowl of cold water for 30 minutes to keep it from drying out. Put the brisket on a plate, cover with plastic wrap, and refrigerate.

3. Continue to gently simmer the broth, adjusting the heat and adding water as needed, until the oxtail meat separates from its bones without resistance, about 4 more hours. Near the end of simmering, soak the rice noodles in a large bowl of warm water for 30 minutes. When they are ready, remove the oxtail and knuckle bones with tongs and set aside to cool, then strain the broth and discard any solids. Return the broth to the stockpot and bring to a simmer, adding salt to taste.

4. Slice the brisket into thin slices and pick out the meat and soft cartilage from the oxtail and knuckle bones. If desired, reserve the bones for making stock. Bring a large pot of water to boil and dip the rice noodles in the boiling water for 30 seconds; remove, strain, and rinse with cold water, then distribute into individual bowls. Distribute the beef pieces among the bowls, then garnish with chopped cilantro, chopped green onions, and onion slices. Ladle the simmering broth into each bowl and serve with Thai basil leaves, lime wedges, and jalapeño slices.

Sukuma Wiki

Collard greens are very versatile and have been in use for at least 2,000 years; the ancient Greeks cultivated them along with kale. Sukuma wiki is the Swahili name for collard greens; it literally translates to "push/stretch the week." As the name implies, collards are available year-round in East Africa and are used to stretch out meals to last all week.

In the culinary world, sukuma wiki is a common name for a Kenyan dish of braised collard greens, usually prepared with ground meat, tomatoes, and onions. I love this dish because it's a breeze to put together and an easy way to put something that tastes slightly exotic on the table on short notice. Make sure to prep your ingredients ahead of time, as this dish comes together quickly.

SERVES: 4

PREP TIME: 10 MINUTES

COOKING TIME: 20 MINUTES

1 TBSP. OLIVE OIL

1/2 WHITE ONION, COARSELY CHOPPED

2 CLOVES GARLIC, CHOPPED

1 JALAPEÑO PEPPER, SEEDED AND CHOPPED

1 LB. GROUND BEEF OR LAMB

1/2 TSP. BLACK PEPPER

1/2 TSP. GROUND CINNAMON

1/2 TSP. GROUND GINGER

1/2 TSP. GROUND FENNEL SEEDS

1/2 TSP. TURMERIC

1 TSP. SEA SALT

1 TSP. GROUND CUMIN

1 TSP. GROUND CORIANDER

1 BUNCH COLLARD GREENS (ABOUT 8 LEAVES), STEMS REMOVED, SLICED INTO 1" STRIPS

1 LARGE HANDFUL (12-15) CHERRY OR GRAPE TOMATOES, QUARTERED

1 TSP. LEMON JUICE

1. Warm the olive oil in a skillet on medium heat, then add the onion. Sauté the onion until softened, about 4 minutes. Add the chopped garlic and jalapeño and sauté until fragrant, about 1 minute. Add the ground beef and seasonings and cook until only slightly pink, about 6 minutes; stir frequently so the ground beef doesn't clump.

2. Add the collard greens and tomatoes and sauté until the collard greens are wilted, about 4 minutes. Stir everything gently as it cooks, being careful not to mush the tomatoes. Add the lemon juice, season with salt and pepper to taste, and serve.

Lamb Tagine

A tagine (sometimes spelled tajine) is a type of slow-cooked Moroccan stew. It gets its name from the earthenware pot in which it is usually cooked, also called a tagine. The use of ceramics in North Africa was the result of Roman influence, so it makes sense that the dish is dated to that period.

A typical tagine is made with a cheaper cut of lamb or beef, like shoulder or shank. Seasonal fruits like dates, raisins, and apricots are often added, along with honey and preserved lemons. Tagine pots are unique in that they trap steam and return the condensed liquid to the dish, enabling chefs to make tender foods with minimal added water, which is ideal in areas where water is scarce.

SERVES: 4

PREP TIME: 10 MINUTES PLUS OVERNIGHT

COOKING TIME: 2 1/2 HOURS

2-3 LBS. LAMB SHOULDER , CUT INTO 1" CHUNKS

1 TSP. GROUND GINGER

2 TSP. BLACK PEPPER

1 TBSP. GROUND CINNAMON

1 TBSP. TURMERIC

1 TBSP. PAPRIKA

1 TBSP. OLIVE OIL

1 TBSP. COCONUT OIL

1 MEDIUM ONION, MINCED

2 TBSP. HARISSA (PAGE 58)

1 TBSP. HONEY

~1 1/2 CUPS CHICKEN BROTH (PAGE 42)

1/2 CUP DRIED APRICOTS

1 TBSP. MINCED PRESERVED LEMON (PAGE 61) OR 1/2 TSP. MINCED LEMON RIND

JUICE OF 1/2 LEMON (1 TBSP.), OR TO TASTE

SLICED ALMONDS, CHOPPED FRESH PARSLEY OR CILANTRO, AND PLAIN YOGURT FOR SERVING

1. Combine the lamb pieces with the ginger, pepper, cinnamon, turmeric, paprika, and olive oil; marinate in the refrigerator overnight.

2. In a Dutch oven or tagine, heat the coconut oil on medium heat. Brown the lamb pieces in batches, turning every few minutes, until well browned and crusted, about 8 minutes per batch. Remove from the pot and set aside when finished.

3. Add the onion to the pot and sauté until aromatic, about 5 minutes, scraping up any chunks of lamb stuck to the bottom. Stir in the harissa and sauté for another 2 minutes. Return the lamb and its juices to the pot, along with the honey and enough chicken broth to mostly cover the lamb, about 1½ cups. Bring to a simmer, then cover, reduce the heat to low, and simmer gently for 1 hour. Add the apricots, simmer for 1 more hour, and check the meat for doneness; a fork should easily pierce the meat. If not done, cover and simmer for another 30 minutes and check again.

4. When the lamb is tender, remove the lamb and apricots with tongs and set aside. Increase the heat to medium-high and reduce the sauce until slightly thickened, about 5 minutes. Return the lamb and apricots to the pot along with the preserved lemon or lemon rind. Season with salt, pepper, and lemon juice to taste, and serve with sliced almonds, chopped parsley or cilantro, and plain yogurt.

Rogan Josh
(Kashmiri Lamb Curry)

Rogan josh is a popular Kashmiri dish that is believed to have originated in Persia before making its way to northern India and beyond. In Persian, rogan means clarified butter and josh means hot or passionate. Its signature red color is historically the result of mild red Kashmiri chiles. Over the years, many restaurants started using tomatoes to give the dish a red color with more easily accessible ingredients. Today, tomato taste has become a part of the dish's profile; my recipe follows the modern interpretation but retains the traditional Kashmiri red chili powder as well.

SERVES: 4
PREP TIME: 10 MINUTES
COOKING TIME: 1 1/2 HOURS

2 BAY LEAVES

6 WHOLE CARDAMOM PODS

1 CINNAMON STICK

1 TBSP. PAPRIKA

1 TBSP. KASHMIRI RED CHILI POWDER (OR 1 TSP. CAYENNE PEPPER)

2 TSP. GROUND CUMIN

1 TSP. SEA SALT

1 TSP. BLACK PEPPER

1 TSP. GROUND CORIANDER

2 MEDIUM ONIONS, COARSELY CHOPPED

1" FRESH GINGER, PEELED AND COARSELY CHOPPED (OR 1 TSP. GROUND GINGER)

8 CLOVES GARLIC, COARSELY CHOPPED

3 WHOLE CLOVES

2 TBSP. GHEE

2-3 LBS. LAMB SHOULDER, CUT INTO 2" CHUNKS

1 (14 OZ.) CAN TOMATO SAUCE

1 LARGE HANDFUL FRESH CILANTRO, COARSELY CHOPPED

1. In a small bowl, combine the bay leaves, cardamom pods, cinnamon stick, paprika, chili powder, cumin, salt, pepper, and coriander, and set aside. In a blender or food processor, blend the onions, ginger, garlic, and cloves into a fine paste.

2. Warm the ghee in a Dutch oven on medium-high heat until shimmering, about 3 minutes. Add the lamb pieces and brown on each side, in batches if needed, turning every 3 minutes. Once the lamb is well browned, reduce the heat to medium and add the onion paste and seasonings, gently stirring to mix the ingredients thoroughly. Sauté until aromatic, about 5 minutes.

3. Stir in the tomato sauce and bring to a simmer. Cover, reduce the heat to low, and simmer for 1 hour. After an hour, remove the lid and check for doneness; the lamb should be fork-tender. If it is still tough, cover and simmer on low for another 30 minutes and then check again, repeating this step as needed until the meat is tender. Add salt and pepper to taste, and fish out any whole cardamom pods you can find.

4. Right before serving, stir in the chopped cilantro. Cilantro is not a traditional accompaniment to this dish, but it adds a nice, fresh-tasting finish. Serve with Steamed Basmati Rice (page 96) or Cauliflower Rice (page 78).

Shashlik
(Russian Shish Kebabs)

Shashlik (Шашлык) is a type of shish kebab commonly found in Russia and the former Soviet republics. It was likely brought to Moscow from central Asia in the 19th century. Today, it's a popular summer food cooked over an open fire at social gatherings. Shashlik is traditionally prepared with lamb, but chicken, pork, and beef variations are becoming increasingly prominent.

I prefer to use metal skewers; the initial investment pays off since you can reuse the skewers and don't have to worry about soaking them ahead of time to prevent burning.

SERVES: 4

PREP TIME: 10 MINUTES, PLUS 4 HOURS TO MARINATE

COOKING TIME: 10 MINUTES

2-3 LBS. LAMB SHOULDER, CUT INTO 2" CHUNKS

2 MEDIUM ONIONS, COARSELY CHOPPED

6 CLOVES GARLIC

1/4 CUP WATER

4 BAY LEAVES

1/4 CUP APPLE CIDER VINEGAR

1 TBSP. BLACK PEPPER

1 TBSP. OREGANO

JUICE OF 1/2 LEMON (1 TBSP.)

4 METAL SKEWERS OR 8 (8") WOODEN SKEWERS

1 TSP. SEA SALT

1. Place the lamb chunks in a resealable plastic bag. Blend the onions, garlic, and water into a smooth purée, then combine with the bay leaves, vinegar, pepper, oregano, and lemon juice. Pour into the bag with the lamb and marinate in the refrigerator for 4 hours. If using wooden skewers, soak them in water for the last hour of marinating time.

2. Remove the lamb from the bag and skewer. Grill on direct high heat, rotating the skewers with tongs every few minutes and sprinkling the salt evenly over the skewers as they cook. The total cooking time should be 8-10 minutes. Let rest for 5 minutes, then serve with sliced fresh vegetables, like tomatoes, mushrooms, or cucumbers. This dish is best enjoyed outdoors with family and friends, as is traditional in Russia.

— CHAPTER 6 —

PORK

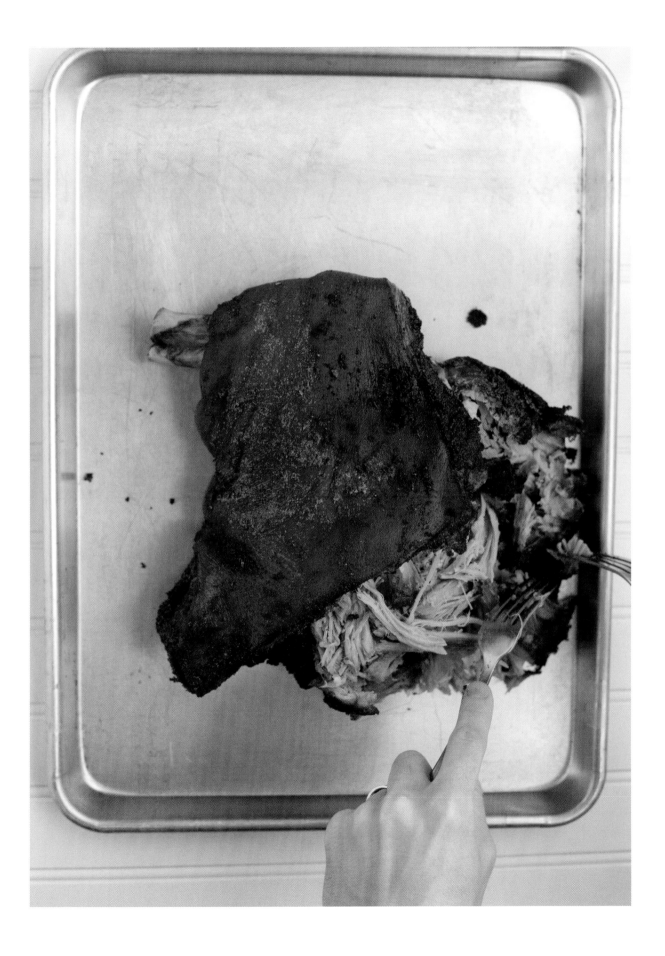

Barbecue Pulled Pork

SERVES: 6

PREP TIME: 1 1/2 HOURS

COOKING TIME: UP TO 16 HOURS

In the pre–Civil War period of the American South, pork became a staple as a low-maintenance and convenient food source; on average, Southerners ate 5 pounds of pork for every pound of beef. While many methods of cooking pork were popular, barbecued pork in the form of pulled pork and ribs (page 170) quickly became a source of Southern identity.

4-8 LBS. PORK BUTT OR SHOULDER (BONE-IN PREFERRED)

1/2 CUP ALL-PURPOSE PORK AND POULTRY RUB (PAGE 47)

HICKORY OR APPLE WOOD CHUNKS, OR A COMBINATION

2 CUPS BARBECUE SAUCE (PAGE 48)

1. Pat the pork dry with paper towels, then rub generously all over with the pork rub. Set out on a baking sheet for 1 hour to come to room temperature as you prepare your grill for indirect smoking (see page 36). Smoke the pork at 225°F until the internal temperature reaches 195-200°F, about 2 hours per pound. The temperature will stall at around 150°F, which is normal. Remove from the grill, wrap in aluminum foil, and let rest in the oven heated to 170°F for at least 30 minutes or up to 1 hour. Remove from the oven and shred the meat with 2 forks or pairs of tongs, discarding any bones. Serve with barbecue sauce.

2. To save fuel, you can remove the pork from the grill once it reaches 150°F, then wrap it in aluminum foil and put it in a 225°F oven to finish. This method creates a less-crusty outside, but the result still tastes good. Check the pork's temperature every 30 minutes until it reaches 195-200°F, which can take upwards of 4 hours depending on the size of your pork shoulder.

Barbecue Ribs

Like pulled pork (page 169), barbecue ribs are a part of Southern culture and identity in the United States. While many cultures have been slow-cooking meats since antiquity, it's the marriage of pork, seasonings, and smoke that gives barbecue ribs their signature flavor and cult following.

While ribs are often smoked upwards of 10 hours at a very low temperature for maximum tenderness, I find that a mid-range temperature produces delicious ribs with a much shorter cooking time.

SERVES: 2-4

PREP TIME: 10 MINUTES, PLUS 1 HOUR TO MARINATE

COOKING TIME: 3-5 HOURS

---

2 RACKS BABY-BACK OR SPARE PORK RIBS

½ CUP ALL-PURPOSE PORK AND POULTRY RUB (PAGE 47)

HICKORY, APPLE, OR CHERRY WOOD CHUNKS, OR A COMBINATION

½ CUP APPLE JUICE

1 CUP BARBECUE SAUCE (PAGE 48)

1. Using a sharp knife and your hands, remove the membrane from the underside of the ribs by cutting it away from the meat and pulling toward the opposite side of the ribs. Removing the membrane takes patience and practice; consult an online video to get the method right.

2. Sprinkle a heavy coating of the pork rub onto the ribs without rubbing it in. Wrap tightly in plastic wrap and refrigerate for 1 hour to allow the rub to melt into the juices that will be released from the salt in the rub.

3. After the ribs have been in the fridge for 30 minutes, prepare your grill for indirect smoking (see page 36). If using a gas grill, prepare as you normally would for indirect smoking, using hickory and/or fruit wood chunks and chips. If using a round charcoal grill, place a large aluminum pan in the center of the grill and fill the grill with unlit charcoal briquettes on both sides of the pan; separately, light a full chimney starter with charcoal briquettes, adding 4 hickory or fruit wood chunks on top. Once the charcoal in the chimney starter is hot, evenly pour the charcoal and wood chunks over the 2 piles of unlit coals. Place the grilling grate on top, cover, and open all vents.

4. Take the ribs out of the plastic wrap and put them on the cool part of the grill. Cover and smoke at 225-250°F for 2½ hours if making baby-back ribs or 3½ hours if making spare ribs. Adjust the ventilation or the gas burners as needed to maintain the desired temperature range.

5. Remove the ribs and wrap each rack tightly with aluminum foil, adding ¼ cup apple juice to each rack. Return to the grill and cook for another 30 minutes. If you're using a charcoal grill, add a few briquettes to each side if needed.

6. Check the ribs for tenderness by piercing the meat with a toothpick; the toothpick should pierce the meat without resistance. If they aren't ready, return the ribs to the grill and check every 30 minutes until done.

7. When they are tender, remove the ribs from their foil wrapping and return to the grill. Brush on some barbecue sauce and cook directly over the flame to caramelize the sauce, about 2 minutes per side. Let rest for 5 minutes and serve.

Meaty Collard Greens

Greens were popular in the early American South when slaves were forced to survive on kitchen scraps like the tops of vegetables and undesirable pork parts, like ham hocks, necks, and feet. Today, the dish has been refined and remains a favorite in many Southern kitchens. In fact, collard greens are the state vegetable of South Carolina.

This recipe is unlike many typical greens recipes, which often add pork or bacon pieces in small portions or as an afterthought; this dish celebrates the savory nature of pork by using both broth and a significant amount of pork. If you aren't able to find smoked ham hocks or neck bones, unsmoked varieties will do—just be sure to add 2 tsp. liquid smoke when adding the greens to the pot. Alternatively, you can buy smoked turkey necks or smoked turkey wings.

SERVES: 6

PREP TIME: 20 MINUTES

COOKING TIME: 3 HOURS

2 LBS. SMOKED HAM HOCKS OR NECK BONES, OR A COMBINATION

1 CUP WATER

2 CUPS CHICKEN OR PORK STOCK (PAGE 42)

2-3 LBS. COLLARD GREENS, TURNIP GREENS, MUSTARD GREENS, OR KALE, OR A COMBINATION, COARSELY CHOPPED WITH STEMS INTACT

1/2 TSP. RED PEPPER FLAKES

1 TBSP. APPLE CIDER VINEGAR

1. Combine the smoked meats, water, and stock in a stockpot over medium heat. Bring to a boil, reduce the heat to medium-low, and gently simmer, uncovered, for 1 hour. Add the greens, red pepper flakes, and vinegar; cover, reduce the heat to low, and simmer for an additional 2 hours or until the leaves are dark green and tear very easily.

2. Fish out the pork pieces with tongs and let cool for a few minutes, then pick out the meat from the bones and skin; return the meat to the pot. Taste and add salt, pepper, and hot sauce if desired—you likely won't need to add salt due to the inherent saltiness of smoked pork.

3. Be sure to drink the leftover, nutrient-dense liquid, known as collard liquor or pot likker; this tradition dates back to Africa.

Pork Adobo

Adobo, often considered the national dish of the Philippines, is a method of stewing meat in vinegar. The word adobo *itself is linked to a Spanish method of preserving raw meat by immersing it in a mixture of vinegar, salt, and paprika. When the Spanish observed an indigenous Philippine cooking method involving vinegar in the 16th century, they referred to it as adobo, and the name stuck. The original name for this dish is no longer known.*

Cane vinegar (sukang maasim) is an integral part of this dish's taste and can be found in any store that carries Philippine products. I keep a bottle of Datu Puti brand at home and use it exclusively to make adobo. White vinegar will work in a pinch.

SERVES: 4

PREP TIME: 2 HOURS TO OVERNIGHT

COOKING TIME: 90 MINUTES

1 1/2 LBS. PORK BELLY, CUT INTO 2" CHUNKS

1 1/2 LBS. PORK SHOULDER, CUT INTO 2" CHUNKS

1/3 CUP TAMARI

10 CLOVES GARLIC, COARSELY CHOPPED

2 TBSP. BLACK PEPPERCORNS

1 TBSP. COCONUT OIL

5 BAY LEAVES

2/3 CUP CANE VINEGAR (WHITE VINEGAR IS OKAY)

1 CUP WATER

1. Combine the pork, tamari, garlic, and peppercorns in a resealable plastic bag and marinate for at least 2 hours, overnight preferred.

2. Warm the coconut oil in a Dutch oven on medium heat for 1 minute, then add the pork pieces and brown, in batches if needed, until a crust forms, turning the pieces every 2-3 minutes. Add the bay leaves, vinegar, and water. Bring to a simmer, cover, reduce the heat to low, and continue to simmer for 1 hour. Do not open the lid during this hour; many people believe that doing so will make the dish taste sour.

3. Remove the pork pieces with tongs and set aside, then strain the liquid and discard the peppercorns, garlic, and bay leaves. (Some cooks prefer to leave them in, which is fine.) Set the liquid aside.

4. Return the pork pieces to the Dutch oven and adjust the heat to medium-low. Sauté the pork until it is crispy and most of the fat has been rendered out, in batches if needed. Turn the pieces every few minutes; it should take about 10 minutes per batch. Set aside the crispy pieces and cover with aluminum foil to keep warm.

5. Return the liquid to the Dutch oven, increase the heat to medium-high, and reduce the liquid by one-third, gently scraping up any remaining pork pieces as the sauce reduces, about 5 minutes. Pour the sauce over the pork and serve with rice (page 96).

Siu Yuk
(Roasted Pork Belly)

Siu yuk (脆皮燒肉) is a Cantonese preparation of roasted pig most often associated with roasted pork belly. This dish is typically reserved for special occasions, like hosting guests or celebrating an accomplishment.

Chinese five-spice powder is sold as a spice mix, but if you are feeling adventurous, you can make it using equal parts star anise, cloves, Chinese cinnamon, Sichuan pepper, and fennel seeds, all ground into a fine powder using a mortar and pestle.

SERVES: 4-6

PREP TIME: 1 HOUR PLUS OVERNIGHT

COOKING TIME: 1 HOUR

2-3 LBS. PORK BELLY (SKIN ON), CUT LENGTHWISE INTO 1 1/2" STRIPS

2 TSP. CHINESE FIVE-SPICE POWDER

2 TSP. WHITE PEPPER

2 TSP. SEA SALT

1. Place the pork belly slices skin side up on a wire rack, and set in the sink. Pour 2 quarts boiling water over the pork belly, then place the rack in the fridge to cool for 1 hour. Combine the seasonings in a small bowl, then rub them all over the 3 meaty sides (not on the skin). Poke the skin all over with a fork. Place the rack back in the fridge and leave to dry, uncovered, overnight.

2. Preheat the oven to 400°F. Place the rack on a baking sheet and roast, skin side up, until the skin is crispy, about 1 hour. Let rest for 5 minutes, then slice and serve. It's easiest to slice pork belly skin side down.

Lemongrass Pork Chops
(Sườn Nướng)

Aside from Pho (page 156) and possibly the vermicelli dish bún, lemongrass pork chops are one of the most identifiable dishes in Vietnamese cuisine. While the combination of fish sauce and pork may sound unappetizing, the finished product is anything but.

For a truly authentic experience, look for thinly sliced pork chops at your local Asian market, or ask your butcher to cut some pork chops to ¼" thickness—one standard American-sized pork chop yields three thin chops.

SERVES: 4

PREP TIME: 10 MINUTES PLUS OVERNIGHT

COOKING TIME: 30 MINUTES

3 STALKS LEMONGRASS, WHITE PARTS ONLY

1 SHALLOT

4 CLOVES GARLIC

2 TBSP. FISH SAUCE

1 TSP. SESAME OIL

1 TSP. SEA SALT

1 TSP. BLACK PEPPER

1 TBSP. LIME JUICE

4 CENTER-CUT BONE-IN PORK CHOPS

1 TBSP. COCONUT OIL

1. In a blender, blend the lemongrass, shallot, garlic, fish sauce, sesame oil, salt, pepper, and lime juice into a paste, adding water if needed. Pierce the pork chops all over with a fork or blade tenderizer, then place in a resealable plastic bag. Add the paste to the pork chops and refrigerate overnight.

2. If using thin-sliced pork chops, grilling is preferred. Grill over direct high heat until cooked through, about 3 minutes per side.

3. Pan-frying creates a tasty crust and is preferred for thicker cuts. Preheat a baking sheet in the oven at 450°F. Heat the coconut oil in a skillet on medium-high heat until shimmering. Sear the pork chops in batches until well browned, 3 minutes per side, then place on the baking sheet in the oven, flipping the chops after 3 minutes. Bake until the internal temperature reaches 135°F, typically 3 minutes per side, but longer if your chops are very thick. If you time it right, you can sear your second batch of pork chops while you bake the first batch. When the pork chops are done baking, tent them with aluminum foil and let them rest for 5 minutes; they will reach 145°F as they rest.

Kalua Pig

*Kalua pig is one of Hawaii's best-known dishes and a lu'au staple. Traditionally, an entire pig is placed in an underground pit (*imu* in Hawaiian) lined with hot rocks; the pork is wrapped in banana leaves, covered with a layer of soil, and roasted overnight. Surprisingly, a slow cooker or Dutch oven and some liquid smoke makes a decent replacement for an imu.*

When selecting a piece of pork for this recipe, look for something with the bone and skin still attached, as it adds a depth of flavor. Pork butt, shoulder, picnic pork, and Boston butt are all from the same area of the pig and work well for this recipe.

SERVES: 6

PREP TIME: 15 MINUTES

COOKING TIME: 14 HOURS

5-7 LBS. PORK BUTT

1 TBSP. COARSE SEA SALT (BLACK OR PINK PREFERRED)

1 TBSP. HICKORY LIQUID SMOKE

1. Place the pork butt in a slow cooker or Dutch oven and pour the sea salt and liquid smoke on top. Cover and cook on low for 14 hours. There is no need to add liquid to the pot. Flip it over halfway through cooking.

2. Pull out the pork pieces with tongs and set them aside, discarding the skin, bone, and any excess fat. Pour the remaining liquid and fat into a fat separator. Place the pork pieces in a pan and gently shred the meat with 2 forks. Pour about half of the defatted liquid back into the pork while you're shredding it.

3. You can reuse the remaining liquid and fat; the liquid makes a great gravy base or pan sauce to pour over any pork roast. Leftover Kalua pig is often mixed with head cabbage, which brings a new texture to the meat and reinvigorates the dish. Reheat the cold pig in a covered pan on medium heat for about 5 minutes, then add chopped cabbage and a little water. Cover and heat for an additional 5 minutes, then serve.

Gamjatang
(Pork Neck Soup)

Gamjatang, a traditional Korean soup, is one of the tastiest ways to eat pork neck, although not the only traditional preparation of this often-overlooked cut. In Southeast Asia, pork neck is usually marinated, grilled, and served with rice; in the Southern United States, it's slow-roasted or used to make Meaty Collard Greens (page 172).

Perilla leaves (ggaennip) and perilla seed powder bring a distinct taste to this dish. Perilla is part of the mint family and is often compared to its Japanese variety, known as shiso. Perilla leaves look like nettle leaves and are often confused with sesame leaves. They are used in pickled dishes and wraps and as garnishes for soups, as in this recipe. If you can't find them at your local Asian market, mint leaves and sesame seed powder are suitable substitutes for perilla leaves and seed powder.

SERVES: 4

PREP TIME: 2 HOURS (TO SOAK THE BONES)

COOKING TIME: 2 HOURS

3 LBS. PORK NECK

1" GINGER, PEELED

1 SMALL ONION

10 BLACK PEPPERCORNS

10 CLOVES GARLIC, DIVIDED

3 TBSP. KOREAN RED PEPPER POWDER

3 TBSP. RICE WINE

3 TBSP. FISH SAUCE

3 TBSP. PERILLA SEED POWDER

1 TSP. GROUND GINGER

4 SMALL RUSSET POTATOES, PEELED

SALT AND BLACK PEPPER TO TASTE

1 BUNCH (1/2 LB.) CHINESE CABBAGE (SUCH AS CHOY SUM OR BOK CHOY)

10 PERILLA LEAVES

5 GREEN ONIONS, CHOPPED

1. Soak the pork neck in cold water for 2 hours, changing the water halfway through. This step helps remove the blood from the bones.

2. In a large stockpot, boil the pork neck for 6 minutes, then drain and rinse with cold water. Rinse out the stockpot as well. Return the pork neck to the stockpot and fill with enough cold water to cover the bones by 1", then add the ginger, whole onion, peppercorns, and 4 cloves garlic. Bring to a boil, reduce the heat to medium-low, and simmer until the meat pulls easily from the bones, about 1½ hours. As it simmers, create your flavoring sauce by blending the Korean red pepper powder, rice wine, fish sauce, perilla seed powder, ground ginger, and the remaining 6 cloves garlic; set aside.

3. Remove the pork neck from the stockpot with tongs and set aside. With a slotted spoon, scoop out the onion, ginger, garlic, and peppercorns. Return the pork neck to the pot; add the blended flavoring sauce and peeled whole potatoes. Season with salt and pepper to taste. Simmer until the potatoes are softened, 15-20 minutes; add the cabbage and perilla leaves, cover, and simmer for an additional 3 minutes. Garnish with green onions and freshly ground black pepper and serve.

Perilla

Lechon Asado
(Cuban Roasted Pork)

SERVES: 6

PREP TIME: 10 MINUTES PLUS OVERNIGHT

COOKING TIME: 8 HOURS

*Lechon asado is a Cuban preparation of roasted pork, often made by roasting an entire pig on a spit (*lechon *translates to "suckling pig"). The traditional marinade uses the juice of bitter oranges, which can be hard to find outside of tropical and subtropical environments. I've found that a mixture of orange and lemon juices is an acceptable substitute and still gives the pork a tangy, delicious taste.*

MARINADE:

10 CLOVES GARLIC

2 TSP. SEA SALT

2 TSP. BLACK PEPPER

1 CUP ORANGE JUICE

1/2 CUP LEMON JUICE

1 MEDIUM ONION, COARSELY CHOPPED

1 TSP. HONEY

1/4 CUP OLIVE OIL

1/2 TSP. DRIED OREGANO

4 LBS. PORK BUTT (BONE-IN, SKIN-ON PREFERRED)

1. Blend the marinade ingredients, then combine with the pork butt in a resealable plastic bag and refrigerate overnight. The next day, remove the pork butt and reserve ¼ cup of the marinade.

2. Prepare your grill for indirect grilling at 230-240°F (see page 36). Place the pork on the cool side of the grill and roast for 3 hours. Flip the pork and brush with marinade, then roast for another 3 hours. Finally, wrap the pork in heavy-duty aluminum foil and pour in the remaining marinade. Roast for 2 more hours or until the internal temperature reaches 190°F.

3. Let the pork rest for 10 minutes in the aluminum foil, then remove the pork, reserving whatever liquid has accumulated. Gently pull the pork apart with 2 forks, pouring on some of the reserved liquid to keep it juicy. For a crispy, carnitas-style texture, lightly sauté the shredded pork in a skillet on medium heat for 5-10 minutes, stirring only occasionally.

Jerk Pork

Jerk is a cooking method and seasoning from Jamaica that typically involves marinating in a paste of allspice (pimento) and Scotch bonnet peppers (often confused with their cousin, the habañero) and cooking over a fire made with pimento wood. Jamaica was first inhabited by the Arwak Indians from South America more than 2,000 years ago. The Arwak brought with them a cooking technique of marinating and drying meat over a fire or in the sun, the basis of beef jerky as we know it today. It also served as the origin of jerk cooking, as in this jerk pork recipe, although the two dishes are wildly different today; beef jerky is a dried, preserved meat, while jerk pork is tender and juicy.

This recipe is a baseline and is only minimally spicy. Add more peppers if you like spicy food.

SERVES: 4

PREP TIME: 5 MINUTES PLUS OVERNIGHT

COOKING TIME: 1 HOUR

MARINADE:

5 GREEN ONIONS

4 CLOVES GARLIC

2 SCOTCH BONNET OR HABAÑERO PEPPERS, SEEDS AND RIBS REMOVED

JUICE OF 1 LIME (2 TBSP.)

1 TBSP. THYME

1 TBSP. ALLSPICE BERRIES

1 TBSP. HONEY

1 TBSP. TOMATO PASTE

2 TSP. SEA SALT

1/2 TSP. GROUND CUMIN

1/2 TSP. GROUND CINNAMON

1/2 TSP. GROUND NUTMEG

1/2 TSP. GROUND GINGER

1 PINCH CLOVES

2-3 LBS. PORK LOIN

1. Combine and blend all the marinade ingredients, adding a little water if the paste gets too thick to purée effectively. Place the pork in a resealable plastic bag, pour the marinade over the pork, and refrigerate overnight.

2. Prepare your grill for direct and indirect grilling (see page 36). Remove the pork from the marinade and set the leftover marinade aside. Grill the pork over direct heat, turning once, until the marinade forms a crust, about 10 minutes. Place on the cool side of the grill and roast using indirect heat, around 300°F, rotating the loin and brushing with the reserved marinade every 10 minutes. When the pork's internal temperature reaches 145°F, after about 30-40 total minutes of cooking, remove from the heat and tent with aluminum foil. Carve after resting for 5 minutes.

Scotch Bonnet

CHAPTER 7

POULTRY AND EGGS

Roasted Chicken

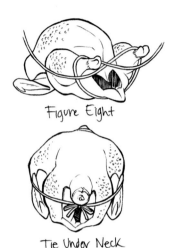

Figure Eight

Tie Under Neck
Divot

SERVES: 3-4

PREP TIME: 1 HOUR 15 MINUTES

COOKING TIME: 1 HOUR

Chickens were first domesticated over 5,000 years ago in South Asia and spread across the world in the years that followed. Initially domesticated for their eggs, the birds themselves weren't eaten until much later. In fact, chicken meat was not a large-scale industry in the United States until the 1920s, when it was promoted as a cheap alternative to beef. Today, chicken is the most popular meat in America.

Inspired by the high-heat roasted chickens prepared in gourmet restaurants all over the world, this whole-bird recipe is the easiest way to make a consistently delicious weeknight dinner. The key to making this foolproof recipe is twofold: You must let the bird come to room temperature, and you must truss it so that it cooks evenly. Both concepts converge to make a perfect roasted bird—a room-temperature bird will cook and crisp quickly without drying out, and trussing eliminates the need to worry about breast versus thigh temperature, as they'll stay the same throughout cooking.

As in my Eye of Round Roast recipe (page 129), if you roast your chicken in a stainless-steel or cast-iron skillet, you can move the skillet onto the stovetop to make a gravy from the drippings without having to transfer the drippings to another pan. This ensures that none of the chicken is wasted and leaves you with one less pan to clean afterward. See page 44 for more information on how to make a gravy using the drippings.

---

1 WHOLE CHICKEN (2-4 LBS.)

1/2 TBSP. KOSHER SALT

1/2 TSP. BLACK PEPPER

1/2 TSP. DRIED THYME

3 CLOVES GARLIC

PEEL OF 1 LEMON OR ORANGE, COARSELY CHOPPED

1 BAY LEAF

30" COOKING TWINE

1. Pat the chicken pat dry inside and out with paper towels. Let the chicken set out for 1 hour to come to room temperature. Preheat the oven to 450°F.

2. Combine the salt, pepper, and thyme. Season the inside of the chicken with one-third of the seasonings, and place the garlic, citrus peel, and bay leaf inside the chicken. Tuck the chicken's wingtips behind the drummettes so that the tip meets the drummette joint that's attached to the body.

3. Truss the chicken by placing the center of the twine under the tail, pulling the twine up and over each drumstick, then looping each end of the twine across the chicken's cavity and under the drumstick, creating a figure-8 shape. Tighten the figure-8 around the legs, then pull the twine down the length of the body, toward the front end, and tie at the front in the notch created by the neck (see illustrations).

4. Sprinkle the remaining seasonings on the outside of the chicken, then place the chicken breast side up in a stainless-steel or cast-iron skillet or on a baking sheet. Roast until the breasts and thighs register 160°F, 50-60 minutes. Remove the twine and let rest for 15 minutes before carving.

Coq au Vin

Coq au vin is often credited to the Burgundy region of France (the same place that gave us the infamous Boeuf Bourguignon), although similar versions may have been eaten during the Roman era. As its French name implies, this dish originally was cooked with a mature rooster and still is today in many parts of France. While historically used to save money (young chickens were more expensive), older chickens created a more complex taste and fared well with an extended braise.

This recipe uses a bouquet garni so that you can easily extract the herbs without disturbing the other ingredients; to make the bouquet, arrange fresh herbs in a single group and tie together with cheesecloth or cooking twine. Skinning pearl onions is a time-consuming process and is often considered a test of patience. For the sake of time, you may want to buy frozen, preskinned pearl onions.

SERVES: 6

PREP TIME: 30 MINUTES (SKINNING THE PEARL ONIONS TAKES A WHILE)

COOKING TIME: 2 HOURS

4 TBSP. BUTTER OR GHEE, DIVIDED

1 WHOLE CHICKEN, QUARTERED (OR 3-5 LBS. BONE-IN, SKIN-ON THIGHS OR LEG QUARTERS)

6 SLICES BACON, DICED

1 LARGE ONION, COARSELY CHOPPED

20 PEARL ONIONS, SKINNED

1 LARGE CARROT, COARSELY CHOPPED

2 SHALLOTS, COARSELY CHOPPED

2 CLOVES GARLIC, SMASHED

BOUQUET GARNI OF FRESH THYME, ROSEMARY, PARSLEY, AND BAY LEAF

1/2 BOTTLE (375 ML) MEDIUM FRUITY RED WINE (BURGUNDY, MERLOT, OR CÔTES DU RHÔNE)

2 CUPS CHICKEN BROTH (PAGE 42)

6 MEDIUM WHITE MUSHROOMS, QUARTERED

1. Preheat the oven to 325°F. In a Dutch oven, melt 2 Tbsp. of the butter or ghee on medium-high heat. Brown the chicken pieces in 2 batches, about 3 minutes per side. Remove the chicken and add the diced bacon, lowering the heat to medium; cook for 2 minutes, then add the onions, carrot, shallots, garlic, and bouquet garni. Sauté until the bacon is cooked through, 6-8 minutes. Add the wine and deglaze the Dutch oven. Add the chicken pieces and broth, cover, and bake for 1 hour.

2. Remove the chicken pieces and place them on a baking sheet. Increase the oven temperature to 400°F and roast the chicken until crisp and brown, 10-20 minutes.

3. As the chicken roasts, strain and reserve the braising liquid and set the solids aside, discarding the bouquet garni. Return the liquid to the Dutch oven and simmer on medium-high heat to reduce by half, about 10 minutes. In a separate skillet, warm the remaining 2 Tbsp. butter for 1 minute on medium heat, then sauté the mushrooms until softened, about 10 minutes.

4. Once the sauce is reduced and the mushrooms are softened, add the mushrooms and braised vegetables to the sauce and gently stir to combine. Add the roasted chicken pieces and serve.

Southern Fried Chicken

SERVES: 6-8

PREP TIME: 5 MINUTES PLUS OVERNIGHT

COOKING TIME: UP TO 1 HOUR

As with many dishes throughout history, the advent of Southern fried chicken was the result of several different events converging. Fried chicken was a West African delicacy brought over to the United States by slaves, the mass production of pork in the South made lard readily available, and the popularity of cast-iron cookware in the 19th century created the fried chicken we now associate with the South.

The key to keeping the chicken moist during frying is to marinate it overnight. Buttermilk imparts a slightly creamy taste to the meat that complements the crispy, savory crust perfectly.

---

4 LBS. BONE-IN, SKIN-ON CHICKEN THIGHS AND/OR DRUMSTICKS

2 CUPS FULL-FAT BUTTERMILK

1 TBSP. SEA SALT

1/4 CUP POTATO STARCH

1/4 CUP TAPIOCA STARCH

1 TSP. SEA SALT

1 TSP. BLACK PEPPER

1 TSP. PAPRIKA

3 CUPS LARD

1. Pat the chicken pieces dry with paper towels. In a resealable plastic bag, combine the chicken, buttermilk, and salt and refrigerate overnight. The next day, drain the chicken in a colander, then let dry on a wire rack over a baking sheet for 30 minutes.

2. Combine the starches and seasonings in a wide, shallow bowl and set aside. Heat the lard in a cast-iron skillet to 340-350°F. Coat the chicken in the seasonings, shaking off the excess, then fry the chicken in batches until the internal temperature reaches 165°F, about 10 minutes per side. Place the cooked chicken on a wire rack over a baking sheet in a warm (170°F) oven as you fry the other pieces.

3. Serve with Dirty Rice (page 100) and Meaty Collard Greens (page 172).

Tandoori Chicken

Tandoori chicken gets its name from the clay oven in which it is traditionally cooked, a tandoor, which dates as far back as the Indus Valley civilization (3000 BC). Marinated in yogurt and spices, this dish is popular in India and beyond and remains one of the most identifiable Indian dishes today.

I always cook two tandoori chickens at once so that I have plenty of leftovers for making Butter Chicken (page 199). Kashmiri red chili powder and garam masala can be found at Asian groceries or online; while you're shopping, be sure to grab some fenugreek leaves and mace, which you'll need for Butter Chicken.

SERVES: 4

PREP TIME: 1 HOUR PLUS OVERNIGHT, PLUS 2 HOURS TO STRAIN THE YOGURT

COOKING TIME: 45 MINUTES

1 WHOLE CHICKEN, QUARTERED (OR 3-5 LBS. BONE-IN THIGHS, LEG QUARTERS, OR SPLIT BREASTS), SKIN AND EXCESS FAT REMOVED

FIRST MARINADE:

1 TSP. SEA SALT

2 TSP. KASHMIRI RED CHILI POWDER

1" GINGER, PEELED

2 CLOVES GARLIC

1 TBSP. LEMON JUICE

SECOND MARINADE:

1 CUP PLAIN YOGURT, STRAINED FOR 2 HOURS

1" GINGER, PEELED AND MINCED

2 CLOVES GARLIC, MINCED

1 TSP. KASHMIRI RED CHILI POWDER

1 TBSP. GARAM MASALA

1 TSP. GROUND CORIANDER

2 TBSP. GHEE, MELTED

1 RED ONION, SLICED INTO RINGS AND SOAKED IN COLD WATER FOR 30 MINUTES

1 LEMON, CUT INTO WEDGES

1. Prep your chicken by slicing deep cuts into the meat to allow the marinades to penetrate it. Also slice across the leg joints and sever the tendon connected to each ankle joint. Blend the first marinade ingredients, then rub them all over the chicken pieces. Place the pieces in a dish, cover, and refrigerate for 30 minutes while you prep the ingredients for the second marinade.

2. Whisk together the ingredients for the second marinade. After 30 minutes, rub the second marinade all over the chicken pieces. Put the chicken in a gallon-sized resealable bag and refrigerate overnight.

3. Cooking over a charcoal or gas grill is preferred. Prep your grill for indirect grilling (see page 36), then grill the chicken pieces bone side down (what would be skin side up if the skin was intact) over direct heat for 10 minutes. Once slightly charred, move to the cool side of the grill and brush with the melted ghee. Continue to grill until the internal temperature of the chicken reaches 160°F, about 30 more minutes.

4. If baking in an oven, place the chicken pieces on a rack set on a rimmed baking sheet and roast at 450°F until cooked through, about 45 minutes. Brush with the melted ghee about 20 minutes into cooking. Serve with red onion slices and lemon wedges.

Butter Chicken
(Murgh Makhani)

Butter chicken is a classic Indian dish and an unforgettable combination of savory, sweet, and rich tastes. It was the first Indian dish I ever tried, in a tiny restaurant in King's Cross, Sydney, and I've been hooked ever since. This dish is surprisingly easy to put together once you have the right ingredients; the most time-consuming part of the recipe is precooking a Tandoori Chicken (page 196).

Butter chicken first appeared in the famous Moti Mahal restaurant in 1920, owned by Kundan Lal Gujral (1903-1997) in the present-day Pakistani city of Peshawar. When India was partitioned in 1947, Gujral relocated the restaurant to Delhi. Today, Moti Mahal has more than 100 franchises in India, and Gujral is credited with inventing the modern recipes for both butter chicken and tandoori chicken.

SERVES: 4

PREP TIME: 10 MINUTES, PLUS TIME TO PREP THE TANDOORI CHICKEN

COOKING TIME: 40 MINUTES

2 TBSP. GHEE

3 CARDAMOM PODS

1 JALAPEÑO, SERRANO, OR OTHER HOT GREEN CHILE, SEEDS AND RIBS REMOVED, JULIENNED

1" GINGER, PEELED AND JULIENNED

3 BLADES MACE (OR 1 TSP. GROUND MACE)

2 CLOVES GARLIC

6 ROMA TOMATOES, CUT INTO BITE-SIZED PIECES

1/2 CUP WATER

3 TBSP. BUTTER

1 TSP. KASHMIRI RED CHILI POWDER

1/2 TSP. GROUND CORIANDER

1/2 TBSP. HONEY

1 TSP. CRUSHED FENUGREEK LEAVES (KASURI METHI)

SALT TO TASTE

1 PRECOOKED TANDOORI CHICKEN (PAGE 196), CUT INTO BITE-SIZED PIECES

1/2 CUP HEAVY CREAM

LEMON WEDGES AND CHOPPED FRESH CILANTRO TO GARNISH

1. Heat the ghee in a large skillet on medium for 1 minute, then add the cardamom pods, chile, ginger, mace, and garlic. Sauté for 1 minute, then add the tomatoes. Sauté until the tomatoes are softened, about 6 minutes. Pour everything into a blender along with the water and blend until smooth, adding more water if it gets too thick. You want the sauce to be the consistency of tomato soup.

2. Return the sauce to the skillet, straining it through a colander (not a fine-mesh strainer, or it'll get stuck) to catch the cardamom shells and tomato skins and create a velvety texture. Stir in the butter, chili powder, and coriander; cover and simmer on medium-low until darkened, about 10 minutes. Add the honey, fenugreek leaves, and salt to taste, again adding more water if the sauce is too thick. Add the chicken pieces, cover, and simmer until warm, about 5 minutes. Remove from the heat and stir in the cream before serving. Serve with Steamed Basmati Rice (page 96), lemon wedges, and chopped fresh cilantro.

Chicken Pad See Ew

Pad see ew (sometimes spelled phat si io) is a Chinese-influenced Thai and Laotian dish made with thick rice noodles. Although it often takes a backseat to its more popular cousin, pad Thai, the balanced sweet and savory taste of pad see ew cannot be overstated. In addition to chicken, this dish can be made with thin slices of pork loin, steak, or shrimp.

The key to flavorful pad see ew, as with many Chinese-style noodle dishes cooked in a wok, is to use a gas burner on high heat. An important consideration when making this dish is either to cook a relatively small amount of ingredients (as in this recipe) or to cook it in batches so as not to cool the wok completely when adding ingredients. The general rule when stir-frying noodles is to make no more than 2 servings at a time.

SERVES: 2

PREP TIME: 40 MINUTES

COOKING TIME: 20 MINUTES

---

8 OZ. WIDE, FLAT RICE NOODLES (CHOW FUN)

1 TBSP. FISH SAUCE

2 TBSP. TAMARI

2 TBSP. COCONUT PALM SUGAR

1 TSP. CHINESE COOKING WINE (SEE PAGE 30)

1 TSP. SHRIMP PASTE (TERASI PREFERRED; SEE PAGE 30)

1/2 TSP. WHITE PEPPER

3 TBSP. COCONUT OIL, DIVIDED

1 EGG, BEATEN

2 CLOVES GARLIC, MINCED

4 CHICKEN THIGHS, THINLY SLICED

8 OZ. (1 SMALL BUNCH) CHINESE CABBAGE (CHOY SUM OR KAI-LAN) OR BROCCOLI, CUT INTO 2" PIECES

1-3 BIRD'S EYE CHILES (DEPENDING ON YOUR HEAT TOLERANCE), SEEDS AND RIBS REMOVED, SLICED

1. Soak the rice noodles in warm water for 30 minutes, then dip into boiling water for 30 seconds. Drain and rinse with cold water, and set aside.

2. Combine the fish sauce, tamari, coconut palm sugar, cooking wine, shrimp paste, and white pepper to make a stir-fry sauce; set aside.

3. In a wok over an open flame, warm 1 Tbsp. of the coconut oil on medium heat, then add the egg. Cook, stirring occasionally, until cooked through and scrambled, then remove the egg and set aside.

4. Add the remaining 2 Tbsp. coconut oil to the wok and increase the heat to high. When the oil is shimmering, add the garlic; sauté until lightly browned, about 15-20 seconds. Add the sliced chicken and stir-fry until mostly cooked through, about 5 minutes, adding 1 Tbsp. of the stir-fry sauce during the last minute of cooking.

5. Add the broccoli and stir-fry until wilted, about 2 minutes. Finally, add the noodles, stir in the rest of the sauce, and toss until well combined but before the noodles start to melt, about 1 minute. Add the egg and sliced chiles, then serve.

Chicken Panang

Panang (also spelled penang and phanaeng) curry is a mild Thai curry that gets its name from the Malaysian island of Penang. It is similar to Thai red curry but is richer and creamier and typically uses crushed peanuts as a major part of the dish. Cashews make a fair substitution.

Panang is often served with pork, chicken, or shrimp in Thai restaurants in the United States, although beef is the traditional meat used in this dish. I love to make this curry with all these meats but typically use chicken for its flavor and texture.

The baseline version of this dish is not spicy; add bird's eye chiles to get to your desired heat profile.

SERVES: 4-6

PREP TIME: 10 MINUTES, PLUS 30 MINUTES TO PREP THE PANANG PASTE

COOKING TIME: 25 MINUTES

2 TBSP. COCONUT OIL

1/4 CUP PANANG PASTE (BELOW)

1 (13.5 OZ.) CAN COCONUT MILK, DIVIDED

2-3 LBS. BONELESS, SKINLESS CHICKEN THIGHS, SLICED INTO BITE-SIZED CHUNKS

1/4 CUP CHOPPED CASHEWS

10 THAI BASIL LEAVES

2 TSP. FISH SAUCE

1 BIRD'S EYE CHILE, SEEDS AND RIBS REMOVED, SLICED INTO RINGS (OPTIONAL)

1. In a skillet, heat the coconut oil on medium heat for 1 minute, then add the Panang Paste, stirring to combine. Sauté until it becomes aromatic and the oil starts to separate from the paste, 3-5 minutes. Add a third of the coconut milk and simmer, stirring often, for another 2 minutes.

2. Add the chicken and stir in another third of the coconut milk. Bring to a simmer, then reduce the heat to medium-low. Simmer, uncovered, until the chicken is nearly cooked through, 8-10 minutes.

3. Add the chopped cashews, Thai basil leaves, fish sauce, and the remaining third of the coconut milk. Add the chile if desired. Raise the heat to medium and simmer for another few minutes until the basil leaves are soft and slightly darkened. Serve with Sticky Rice (page 99) or Cauliflower Rice (page 78).

PANANG PASTE

YIELDS: 1 CUP

3 LARGE DRIED MILD RED CHILES (SUCH AS GUAJILLO OR ANAHEIM)

1 TSP. CORIANDER SEEDS, TOASTED

1 TSP. CUMIN SEEDS, TOASTED

3" LEMONGRASS (WHITE BASE OF 1 STALK), COARSELY CHOPPED

2" GALANGAL, PEELED AND COARSELY CHOPPED

5 FRESH KAFFIR LIME LEAVES

1 TSP. SHRIMP PASTE (TERASI PREFERRED; SEE PAGE 30)

2 GREEN CARDAMOM PODS

2 SMALL SHALLOTS

2 CLOVES GARLIC

1 TBSP. SEA SALT

1 TSP. BLACK PEPPERCORNS

1/4 CUP COARSELY CHOPPED CASHEWS

1 TBSP. WATER

1. Soak the chiles in warm water for 30 minutes, then remove the stems and seeds. Blend or process the chiles with the remaining ingredients.

2. This paste will keep in the fridge for up to 2 weeks or in the freezer for up to 6 months. Before freezing, divide the paste into ¼ cup portions.

Chicken Satay

Originally from Indonesia, satay (often spelled sate) can be found in many Asian restaurants as an appetizer. Satay was first sold by street vendors on Java island, probably an adaptation of Indian-style kebabs, a result of Indian and Middle Eastern migration to Indonesia in the 18th and 19th centuries. From there, the dish moved to other Indonesian islands and beyond. Satay is commonly made with chicken, beef, lamb, and shrimp. More exotic variations include turtle, crocodile, lizard, snake, and rabbit.

SERVES: 6-10

PREP TIME: 10 MINUTES PLUS OVERNIGHT

COOKING TIME: 20 MINUTES

MARINADE:

2 STALKS LEMONGRASS, WHITE PARTS ONLY, CHOPPED (~1 CUP)

2 SHALLOTS

4 CLOVES GARLIC

1/2" GALANGAL, PEELED

1/2" GINGER, PEELED

2/3 CUP COCONUT MILK

2 TBSP. COCONUT OIL

2 TBSP. HONEY

2 TSP. GROUND CORIANDER

1 TSP. SEA SALT

1/2 TSP. TURMERIC

3-5 LBS. BONELESS, SKINLESS CHICKEN BREASTS, SLICED LENGTHWISE INTO 1" STRIPS

20 (8") WOODEN SKEWERS

SATAY SAUCE (PAGE 62)

1. Blend all the marinade ingredients, adding water if the paste is difficult to purée. Combine the paste and chicken in a resealable plastic bag and refrigerate overnight.

2. Soak the skewers in water for 1 hour. Remove the chicken from the bag and reserve the marinade. Skewer the chicken in a weaving pattern, making a weave every 1". Grill the chicken on direct medium-high heat, turning every few minutes, brushing on the reserved marinade as you turn the chicken. It should take 8 minutes total. Let rest for 5 minutes, then serve with satay sauce.

Teriyaki Chicken

SERVES: 4

PREP TIME: UP TO 4 HOURS, PLUS
TIME TO PREP THE TERIYAKI SAUCE

COOKING TIME: 20 MINUTES

Teriyaki is a popular Japanese cooking technique in which meat is basted while being grilled. As I mention in my Teriyaki Sauce recipe (page 64), it was developed in the 17th century and is often made with fish, chicken, beef, or squid.

1 RECIPE TERIYAKI SAUCE (PAGE 64)

6-8 BONELESS, SKINLESS CHICKEN THIGHS

SESAME SEEDS FOR SERVING

1. Prepare the Teriyaki Sauce and let cool. Reserve ½ cup of the sauce. Marinate the chicken thighs in the remaining sauce for 2-4 hours.

2. Prepare your grill for indirect grilling (see page 36). Place the chicken over direct high heat, brush with the marinade, and grill until browned, about 5 minutes. Flip the chicken and brush again, grilling for another 5 minutes or until the other side is browned.

3. Move the chicken to the cool side of the grill to finish cooking; the internal temperature should reach 160°F. Brush with the reserved sauce before serving with sesame seeds sprinkled on top.

Yakitori

Yakitori (literally, "grilled chicken") is a Japanese cooking technique that involves skewering and grilling foods. Going to a yakitori-ya (restaurant) or food stand on an empty stomach can be less than healthy for your wallet; making yakitori at home is much more affordable and is a great way to entertain guests or enjoy a dinner for two. This meal can easily be scaled up to meet your needs.

The only tricky part of this recipe is making the meatballs; ground chicken tends to be difficult to grill. I found success by partially cooking the meatballs in a pan before skewering and finishing them off on the grill. Feel free to add other foods to the skewers, such as garlic cloves, asparagus, chicken thigh strips, skin, wings, tails, and livers.

SERVES: 2

PREP TIME: 10 MINUTES, PLUS 1 HOUR TO SOAK THE SKEWERS

COOKING TIME: 20 MINUTES

CHICKEN MEATBALLS:

15 (8") WOODEN SKEWERS

1 TBSP. BUTTER

1/2 SMALL ONION, BLENDED IN A BLENDER OR FOOD PROCESSOR

1/2 LB. GROUND CHICKEN

1 SMALL FRESH SHIITAKE MUSHROOM, MINCED

1/4 TSP. LEMON ZEST

1 TSP. SEA SALT

1 TBSP. COCONUT OIL

6 CHICKEN GIZZARDS

10 CHICKEN HEARTS

4 SHIITAKE MUSHROOMS

6 GREEN ONIONS, CUT INTO 2" LENGTHS

1/2 RECIPE YAKITORI SAUCE (PAGE 64; SEE YAKITORI VARIATION AT END), PLUS 1/4 CUP FOR DIPPING

SESAME SEEDS TO GARNISH

1. Soak the skewers in water for 1 hour. Melt the butter in a skillet on medium heat, then add the blended onion. Sauté until softened, about 2 minutes, then transfer to a bowl to cool. Add the ground chicken, shiitake mushroom, lemon zest, and salt to the bowl, then form into 8 or 9 balls. Warm the coconut oil in a skillet on medium-high heat until shimmering, about 2 minutes, then add the meatballs and lightly brown on each side to help them keep their form. Do not cook through. Set aside to cool, then skewer with soaked wooden skewers.

2. Skewer the gizzards, hearts, shiitake mushrooms, and green onions, as well as any other foods you'd like.

3. Prepare your grill for direct cooking (see page 36). Grill the skewers over direct high heat, turning every couple minutes and basting with yakitori sauce as you turn them. Garnish with sesame seeds and serve with sesame salt powder (known as gomashio; see recipe below) and more yakitori sauce for dipping.

GOMASHIO

1 TBSP. SESAME SEEDS

1 TSP. KOSHER SALT

1. Grind the seeds and salt together with a mortar and pestle.

Roasted Duck and Potatoes

Wild ducks have been consumed since prehistory, but the Chinese claim to have domesticated ducks first, more than 3,000 years ago. Europeans weren't far behind; the Romans maintained aviaries that included ducks. Separately, Native Americans recognized the tastiness of ducks and domesticated them before the arrival of Western Europeans.

For my recipe, I wanted to highlight the natural deliciousness of this bird with minimal fuss (although to be fair, cooking duck is easier than cooking chicken because duck's dark meat is much less likely to dry out). In truth, the real stars of this recipe are the potatoes, which are roasted in the duck's rendered fat; they may be the tastiest potatoes you've ever eaten. Other root vegetables, including carrots, parsnips, and turnips, can be mixed with the potatoes to delicious effect. Finishing the fatty bird with lemon juice adds another taste dimension.

SERVES: 4

PREP TIME: 40 MINUTES

COOKING TIME: 3 HOURS

1 WHOLE DUCK (3-5 LBS.)

1 TSP. KOSHER SALT

1 TSP. BLACK PEPPER

1/2 ONION, QUARTERED

5 SPRIGS THYME

5 FRESH SAGE LEAVES

2 LBS. RUSSET POTATOES (4-5), PEELED AND QUARTERED

JUICE OF 1/2 LEMON (1 TBSP.)

1. Pat the duck dry inside and out with paper towels. Trim any extra skin and fat from both openings and reserve for rendering (see pages 40-41). If there is a neck attached, cut it at the base of the shoulder and reserve for making broth (see page 42). Set the duck on a roasting rack or wire rack to air-dry for 30 minutes. As the duck dries, preheat the oven to 350°F.

2. Pierce the duck skin (not the meat) all over with a fork, then cover with the salt and pepper. Stuff the onion quarters and herbs into the cavity. Suspend the duck over a baking sheet on the roasting rack—the higher the better—then place in the oven to roast for 1 hour. I like to dust the giblets (heart, liver, and gizzards) with tapioca starch and pan-fry them in butter to eat while the duck is roasting.

3. After 1 hour, toss the peeled and quartered potatoes in a little kosher salt, then add them to the baking sheet; turn them so they are covered in the rendered duck fat. Reduce the oven temperature to 300°F and roast until the thigh meat registers 165°F, about 1 hour 20 minutes. Broil the duck for 1 minute if it doesn't appear crispy. Remove from the oven and place the duck on a separate baking sheet to rest. Meanwhile, increase the oven temperature to 450°F and roast the potatoes until golden brown, 20-40 minutes. They should be swimming in delicious duck fat at this point; carefully flip the potatoes at the 10-minute mark and again if needed. After the duck has rested for 20 minutes, carve and serve with the potatoes, seasoning with lemon juice and a little salt right before presenting.

Smoked Turkey Legs

Although smoked turkey legs are largely relegated to theme parks and renaissance fairs today, they have a fairly rich and long-standing history. Turkeys were a product of the New World and became popular in England in the 16th century. Back then, breasts were considered prized cuts of the bird, and legs were left over and sold to the general populace, especially during street fairs. So the tradition was born.

This recipe is similar to the legs you'll find at fairs today, except that many places soak their turkey legs in sodium nitrate overnight to give them their signature pink color and cured flavor. I don't have any issues with sodium nitrate in particular (the use of curing salts has been deemed safe by many respected nutritionists), but I find it to be an unnecessary step when cooking at home.

SERVES: 4

PREP TIME: UP TO 24 HOURS

COOKING TIME: UP TO 5 HOURS

5 CUPS WATER, DIVIDED

1/2 CUP KOSHER SALT

1/4 CUP HONEY

1 TBSP. PAPRIKA

1/2 TBSP. ONION POWDER

1/2 TBSP. GARLIC POWDER

1/2 TBSP. BLACK PEPPER

1/2 TSP. CAYENNE PEPPER

4 ALLSPICE BERRIES

1 CUP ICE CUBES

4 TURKEY LEGS

1. Bring 3 cups of the water and all the seasonings to a boil, then stir in the remaining 2 cups cold water and ice cubes. Stir until the ice melts to bring the mixture to room temperature, adding more ice if needed. Put the turkey legs in gallon-sized plastic bags, 2 legs per bag, then pour the brine evenly into each bag. Let soak in the brine in the refrigerator overnight.

2. The next day, pour out and discard the brine, then rinse and pat dry the turkey legs. Prepare your grill for indirect smoking using cherry or apple wood (see page 36). Smoke at 245-260°F until the internal temperature reaches 165°F, 3-5 hours. Allow to rest for 5 minutes, then serve.

Sephardic Jewish-Style Roasted Eggs
(Huevos Haminados)

This egg dish is popular in Jewish communities in the Middle East and the Mediterranean and is served at Passover Seders (a ritual feast that marks the beginning of Passover). The dish's Latin-based name might throw you off, but it's a reflection of its origin in medieval Spain. There are several variations, which include boiling the eggs in onion skins and coffee or simmering them in a slow cooker for several hours. I have found that roasting the eggs directly in the oven is the simplest and most rewarding method.

While the eggshells stay mostly white, the whites become a rich brown color, and the eggs develop a nutty, roasted taste. This cooking method also imparts a hint of meatiness that's difficult to describe but delicious nonetheless.

SERVES: 4

COOKING TIME: 5 HOURS

8 EGGS

1. Preheat the oven to 220°F, then place the eggs directly on the oven rack and roast for 5 hours. There is no need to rotate the eggs. Some of the whites will make their way through the shells, creating dark spots on the shells, which is fine. Place a sheet of aluminum foil under the eggs in case an egg cracks (which is unlikely).

2. After 5 hours, place the eggs in a bowl of cold water for 5 minutes. Then crack them open and enjoy; the eggs will have shrunk significantly and will be a dream to peel.

215

Shakshouka

Shakshouka is a popular North African dish of eggs poached in tomatoes and peppers. Its origin is the subject of debate; some believe that it came from Turkey, where they have a similar dish called menemen, while others believe that it has roots in Yemen. Regardless, Tunisia is generally considered the birthplace of shakshouka as we know it today. Because of its use of eggs, it's usually served at breakfast, although in Israel it is sometimes served for dinner.

The combination of tomatoes, peppers, and eggs is a naturally tasty union, as evidenced by its prevalence all over the world. In addition to North Africa and the Middle East, the combination is popular in the Americas—the most popular version of all being huevos rancheros.

SERVES: 2
PREP TIME: 10 MINUTES
COOKING TIME: 40 MINUTES

2 TBSP. OLIVE OIL

2 ONIONS, SLICED

2 RED BELL PEPPERS, SLICED LENGTHWISE INTO 1/2" STRIPS

1 TSP. GROUND CUMIN

1 TSP. GROUND CORIANDER

2 BAY LEAVES

2 TBSP. TOMATO PASTE

2 TBSP. HARISSA (PAGE 58)

1 (28 OZ.) CAN WHOLE PEELED TOMATOES

4 EGGS

1/2 CUP THICK PLAIN YOGURT

1 SMALL HANDFUL FRESH PARSLEY, CHOPPED

1. Heat the olive oil in a skillet on medium for 1 minute. Add the sliced onions and sauté until softened, about 6 minutes. Add the bell pepper strips and sauté until softened, about 8 minutes, stirring occasionally. Add the cumin, coriander, bay leaves, tomato paste, and harissa and sauté until fragrant, about 2 minutes. Add the tomatoes and simmer until thickened, about 15 minutes, stirring occasionally.

2. When the tomato sauce is ready, crack the eggs on top and cook to your liking. Add a few dollops of yogurt, carefully stir it around to incorporate, garnish with the parsley, then serve with the remaining yogurt.

Steamed Eggs
(Gaeran Jim)

I often tire of making eggs in the typical Western style and find steamed eggs to be an excellent change of pace. This recipe is modeled after the Korean preparation of this dish. It's dead-simple and delicious. In Korea, they often use salted shrimp to bring umami flavors to the dish; I find that fish stock or dashi works well, without having to shop for an extra ingredient.

You can scale the dish to serve more people if you have a larger pot, but the cooking time will probably be a bit longer. The trick is to simmer as gently as possible, which creates an appealing texture and ensures that the bottom doesn't burn.

SERVES: 2
PREP TIME: 5 MINUTES
COOKING TIME: 10 MINUTES

1/2 CUP FISH STOCK (PAGE 42) OR DASHI (PART OF THE NABEMONO RECIPE, PAGE 256)

2 EGGS, BEATEN

1/2 TSP. FISH SAUCE

2 GREEN ONIONS, FINELY CHOPPED, DIVIDED

1. If you have an earthenware bowl (ddukbaegi), you can steam the eggs directly over a fire as pictured. If you don't have an earthenware bowl, you can make this dish in a small pot. Bring the stock or dashi to a boil, then reduce the heat to low until it is barely simmering. As it heats, whisk together the beaten eggs, fish sauce, and all but a few pinches of green onion in a separate bowl. Once the broth is simmering, add the egg mixture to the earthenware bowl and stir for 10 seconds, then cover and steam on low until cooked through, 4-5 minutes. Garnish with the remaining green onions.

2. Alternatively, you can steam the eggs in a water bath for a silkier, custard-like texture. Combine all the ingredients (reserving some green onion) in a heat-safe ceramic bowl, whisk until frothy, and place the bowl in a pot. Fill the pot with hot water until it's halfway up the bowl, then cover and steam on low until the eggs are cooked through, 10-12 minutes. Carefully remove the bowl and garnish with the remaining green onions.

3. This dish can also be made in a microwave. Combine all the ingredients (reserving some green onion) in a microwave-safe bowl and microwave for 3 minutes. Check for doneness, and microwave for another minute if needed. It won't be as pretty, but it'll still taste good. Garnish with the remaining green onions.

Son-in-Law Eggs

The history behind this dish is frequently debated, but there's no mistaking the fact that it is a true Thai dish, with its use of tamarind, lime, fish sauce, and hot chiles. It is typically made with soft-boiled eggs, but I find the process of peeling a soft-boiled egg to be no fun. A medium-boiled egg still produces the gooey yolk that's a signature part of this dish, and peeling is exponentially easier. Bear in mind that older eggs are easier to peel than fresh eggs.

SERVES: 4

PREP TIME: 10 MINUTES

COOKING TIME: 40 MINUTES

2 SHALLOTS

4 TBSP. COCONUT OIL

1 TBSP. TAMARIND PASTE

2 TBSP. HOT WATER

2 TBSP. HONEY

1 TBSP. FISH SAUCE

1 TBSP. LIME JUICE

2 CLOVES GARLIC, MINCED

2 BIRD'S EYE CHILES, SEEDS AND RIBS REMOVED, SLICED

1/2 CUP WATER

1 TBSP. ARROWROOT STARCH

1 TBSP. COLD WATER

8 COLD EGGS

1 SMALL HANDFUL FRESH CILANTRO, CHOPPED

1. Make crispy fried shallots by thinly slicing the shallots with a mandoline or knife, then pan-frying in the coconut oil on medium-high heat, stirring constantly. Once they turn golden brown, about 2-3 minutes, transfer the shallots to a plate lined with paper towels to dry. You should have ½ cup fried shallots. Strain and reserve the oil.

2. Stir the tamarind paste into 2 Tbsp. hot water to liquefy; strain out any chunks of shell and discard. Combine the tamarind, honey, fish sauce, lime juice, garlic, chiles, and ½ cup water in a saucepan and bring to a simmer on medium-low heat. Mix the arrowroot starch with 1 Tbsp. cold water in a small bowl to create a slurry, then stir it into the sauce. Return the sauce to a simmer and allow to thicken, adding water if it gets too thick. Reduce the heat to low and keep the sauce warm as you prepare the eggs.

3. Using a slotted spoon, carefully add the eggs to a pot of boiling, salted water. Gently boil for 6½ minutes, then spoon the eggs into a bowl of ice water; allow to cool, about 5 minutes. Carefully peel the eggs.

4. In a skillet, heat 2 Tbsp. of the reserved coconut oil on medium-high heat until shimmering, about 2 minutes. Fry the eggs 2 at a time, gently rolling them back and forth constantly with a spoon. It'll take about 4 minutes per egg; once finished, set the eggs on paper towels to drain. Add more oil if needed. Serve the eggs drizzled with sauce and sprinkled with fried shallots and chopped cilantro.

CHAPTER 8

SEAFOOD

Pesce al Sale
(Salt-Crusted Fish)

SERVES: 2

PREP TIME: 20 MINUTES

COOKING TIME: 25 MINUTES

This Italian favorite is the perfect date-night dish; in just a few steps you can have a perfectly cooked fish that's a novelty to reveal to your dinner companion. It remains a common way of cooking fish in Sicily. Be sure to crack the crust and serve the fish directly on the serving table for the most impressive results. Honestly, I think it's just as fun to put the salt on fish as it is to take it off.

1 LEMON

1-2 LBS. WHOLE FIRM FISH (RED SNAPPER, TROUT, ROCK COD, OR SEA BASS), CLEANED, SCALED, HEAD INTACT

2 SPRIGS FRESH DILL

2-3 LBS. COARSE SEA SALT (KOSHER SALT IS OKAY)

3 EGG WHITES

HIGH-QUALITY OLIVE OIL FOR DRIZZLING

1. Preheat the oven to 450°F. Cut half of the lemon into slices and the other half into wedges for serving. Stuff the fish with the lemon slices and dill. Combine the salt and egg whites in a large mixing bowl.

2. Spread one-third of the salt mixture on a large rimmed baking sheet until it covers an area 1" wider than the fish. Place the fish on the salt base, then cover the fish evenly with the remaining salt.

3. Bake for 22-25 minutes. You'll know that the fish is done when the salt has formed a nice brown ring around it and you can insert a paring knife into the center of the crust with little resistance. Let it rest for 5 minutes, then crack open the salt crust with a spoon or wooden mallet. Drizzle with olive oil and serve with lemon wedges.

Chinese Steamed Sea Bass

SERVES: 2

PREP TIME: 10 MINUTES

COOKING TIME: 10 MINUTES

Chinese steamed sea bass is a popular Cantonese dish and an excellent way to celebrate the tastiness of fresh ingredients with minimal preparation or fuss.

1-2 LBS. SEA BASS OR OTHER WHOLE WHITE FISH, CLEANED, SCALED, HEAD INTACT

1" GINGER, PEELED AND JULIENNED

2 GREEN ONIONS, THINLY SLICED

1/2 TSP. CHILI POWDER

2 TBSP. CHINESE COOKING WINE (SEE PAGE 30)

2 TBSP. TAMARI

2 TSP. SESAME OIL

1. Preheat the oven to 350°F. Rinse the fish in cold water and pat dry with paper towels. Place the fish on the center of a piece of aluminum foil large enough to wrap around the fish. Sprinkle on the ginger, green onions, and chili powder, then pour the wine, tamari, and sesame oil over the fish.

2. Seal the fish in the foil, place it on a baking sheet, and bake for 10 minutes. Unwrap and check to see if the fish is fully cooked; it should slightly resist pulling away from the bone since it will cook a little more off the heat. Return it to the oven if it needs more time; otherwise, let it sit for 2 minutes wrapped in the foil. Unwrap and transfer to a serving dish, pouring the leftover sauce over the fish before serving.

Sole Meunière

Sole meunière is a classic French dish and an easy inclusion in this cookbook; Julia Child, best known for introducing gourmet French cuisine to the United States, had what she considered to be a "culinary revelation" when she first tasted this dish. It's easy to see why, as the combination of mild white fish, browned butter, and lemon is basic but striking and never gets old.

While sole is the traditional fish used in this dish, any flatfish will work fine, like plaice, turbot, or flounder. Each of these fish has four fillets, a unique characteristic of all flatfish.

SERVES: 2

PREP TIME: 5 MINUTES

COOKING TIME: 8 MINUTES

2 SOLE, PLAICE, TURBOT, OR FLOUNDER FILLETS, ABOUT 6 OZ. EACH

1/4 TSP. SEA SALT

1/4 TSP. FRESH-GROUND BLACK PEPPER

3 TBSP. TAPIOCA STARCH OR ARROWROOT STARCH

2 TBSP. COCONUT OIL

2 TBSP. BUTTER

1 LEMON, SLICED

1. Gently rinse and pat dry the fillets with paper towels. Sprinkle both sides with salt and pepper. Dredge the fish in the starch on both sides, shaking off the excess. Place on a plate and set aside.

2. Heat the coconut oil in a large skillet on medium-high until shimmering, about 2 minutes, then stir in the butter. When the butter stops foaming (about 40 seconds), add the fish and pan-fry until golden brown, about 3 minutes. Carefully flip the fish and cook until done, another 2-3 minutes, adding the lemon slices during the last 20 seconds of cooking. Pour the browned butter and lemon sauce over the fillets when serving.

Blackened Fish

Most often associated with Cajun cuisine, blackening is a cooking method in which a food is coated in spices and cooked in a very hot cast-iron skillet, creating a black crust from the charred spices. This dish became especially admired in the 1980s when popular Cajun chef Paul Prudhomme introduced his recipe to the world.

This dish is best cooked outdoors on a portable gas burner. If you make it indoors, be sure to open your windows and turn on any vent fans you have. This dish goes well with Dirty Rice (page 100) and Meaty Collard Greens (page 172).

SERVES: 2
PREP TIME: 5 MINUTES
COOKING TIME: 20 MINUTES

1 TBSP. PAPRIKA

1 TSP. GARLIC POWDER

1 TSP. ONION POWDER

1 TSP. BLACK PEPPER

1 TSP. SEA SALT

1 TSP. DRIED THYME

1 TSP. CELERY SALT

2 FIRM FISH FILLETS (CATFISH, SALMON, SNAPPER, REDFISH, OR TROUT)

2 TBSP. GHEE

1. Combine the spices, then sprinkle evenly over both sides of the fillets; gently press the spices into the fish with your hands.

2. Heat a cast-iron skillet over high heat until it starts to smoke and the inside starts to turn white, about 5 minutes. Add the ghee, then immediately add the fillets; sear for 2 minutes, then carefully flip and pan-fry until cooked through, 1-2 more minutes.

Fish Pie

Fish pie is a traditional British dish, not unlike Shepherd's Pie (page 131). Fish pies have been a part of British cuisine since the Middle Ages, when lamprey pies were especially prized by the upper classes throughout most of Europe. This dish was originally prepared with a pastry crust, but the introduction of potatoes from the New World in the 16th century led to mashed potatoes becoming the signature topping.

SERVES: 4

PREP TIME: 20 MINUTES

COOKING TIME: 2 HOURS

2 LBS. RUSSET OR YUKON GOLD POTATOES, PEELED AND CUT INTO 1" CHUNKS

7 TBSP. BUTTER, DIVIDED

SALT AND BLACK PEPPER TO TASTE

1 1/2 CUPS HEAVY CREAM

1 CUP CHICKEN STOCK OR BROTH (PAGE 42)

1 BAY LEAF

1 SMALL HANDFUL FRESH PARSLEY, STEMS AND LEAVES SEPARATED

1/2 LB. SALMON FILLET, CUT INTO LARGE CHUNKS

1/2 LB. WHITE FISH (LIKE COD), CUT INTO LARGE CHUNKS

1/2 LB. SMOKED FISH (LIKE TROUT, HADDOCK, OR MACKEREL), CUT INTO LARGE CHUNKS

1/2 LB. RAW SHRIMP, PEELED AND DEVEINED

3 TBSP. WHITE RICE FLOUR

1. Place the potatoes in a large stockpot and fill with enough water to cover the potatoes by 1". Bring to a boil, reduce the heat to medium, and simmer until fork-tender, about 15 minutes. Drain and mash with 4 Tbsp. of the butter until smooth, seasoning with salt and pepper to taste, then set aside.

2. Preheat the oven to 350°F, arranging the racks so that one is in the center of the oven and one is underneath it. Place the cream, stock, bay leaf, and parsley stems in a large skillet and bring to a simmer on low. Add the seafood and gently simmer until nearly cooked through, about 10 minutes. Strain, reserving the liquid. Set aside the seafood and remove and discard the bay leaf and parsley stems.

3. Clean your skillet and return it to the stove. Heat the remaining 3 Tbsp. butter over medium heat, add the flour, and toast until golden brown, about 4 minutes. Slowly add the reserved poaching liquid, whisking continuously until you have a thick white sauce. Simmer over low heat for 5 minutes, adding more cream or stock if it gets too thick. Coarsely chop the parsley leaves, add them to the sauce, and season with salt and pepper to taste. Remove from the heat and carefully add the cooked seafood.

4. Place the mixture in a large pie pan or baking dish and cover with the mashed potatoes. Place a sheet of aluminum foil on the bottom oven rack. Bake the pie on the center rack for 40 minutes or until topping is golden brown and the sauce is beginning to bubble up around the sides.

Lomi Lomi Salmon

SERVES: 4

PREP TIME: 5 MINUTES PLUS OVERNIGHT

COOKING TIME: 10 MINUTES

While the combination of raw fish and fresh ingredients found in lomi lomi salmon would lead you to think that this dish is a long-standing tradition in Hawaii, the truth is that it was introduced to the Hawaiians by early Western sailors. Lomi lomi itself translates to "massage," signifying the mixing of ingredients (usually with bare hands) at the end.

2 TSP. SEA SALT, DIVIDED

8 OZ. SALMON FILLET

2 TOMATOES, SEEDED AND DICED

1 SWEET ONION, DICED

3 GREEN ONIONS, SLICED

1. On a plate, spread 1 tsp. of the sea salt and place the salmon over it. Rub the remaining 1 tsp. sea salt on the top of the salmon, cover with plastic wrap, and refrigerate overnight.

2. The next day, rinse and pat dry the salmon fillet. Cut the salmon into small cubes, then mix with the cut vegetables. Serve cold.

Caldo de Camarón
(Mexican Shrimp Soup)

Caldo de camarón has its roots in pre-Colombian times; a similar Aztec dish called tlaxtihuilli was well documented before the arrival of Western explorers. While tlaxtihuilli is usually thickened with corn dough, caldo de camarón is thinner and highlights the fresh ingredients used in the soup.

Using shell-on shrimp adds intense flavor to the soup, although a soup made with shelled shrimp is easier to eat and tastes fine as well. Alternatively, you could shell the shrimp yourself, simmer the shells and heads in the fish broth for 20 minutes, and then strain. This method gives you the best of both worlds—a robust shrimp taste and a soup that's easy to eat.

SERVES: 4

PREP TIME: 30 MINUTES

COOKING TIME: 40 MINUTES

2 LARGE DRIED MILD CHILES (ANAHEIM, GUAJILLO, ANCHO, OR A COMBINATION)

1 MEDIUM ONION

2 CLOVES GARLIC

1 TSP. DRIED OREGANO

1 (14.5 OZ.) CAN WHOLE, PURÉED, CRUSHED, OR DICED TOMATOES

2 CUPS FISH BROTH (PAGE 42)

1 CUP WATER

2 BAY LEAVES

2 CARROTS, DICED

1 LB. RAW SHRIMP, SHELL-ON PREFERRED

JUICE OF 1/2 LIME (1 TBSP.)

1/4 TSP. SEA SALT

1/4 TSP. BLACK PEPPER

HOT SAUCE, CHOPPED CILANTRO, AND LIME WEDGES FOR SERVING

1. Soak the chiles in warm water for 30 minutes, then cut off the stems and remove the seeds.

2. In a blender, blend the chiles, onion, garlic, oregano, and tomatoes into a smooth puree. Add the puree to a stockpot, cover, and simmer on medium-low until aromatic, about 6 minutes. Cover the pot to prevent splattering. Add the broth, water, and bay leaves and simmer, uncovered, for 20 minutes to darken and allow the flavors to marry.

3. After 20 minutes, pour the soup through a large-holed strainer or colander to collect large chunks of chili skin, then return the soup to the pot. Return to a simmer on medium-low, add the carrots, and simmer for 5 minutes. Add the shrimp and simmer for 3 more minutes, then turn off the heat, cover, and let it sit for 7 minutes. This will allow the flavor to penetrate the shrimp without overcooking it.

4. Prior to serving, add the lime juice, salt, and pepper. Remove the bay leaves and serve with hot sauce, chopped cilantro, and lime wedges.

Shrimp Ceviche

Ceviche is a popular seafood dish in Central and South America made from raw seafood (usually fish or shrimp) marinated in citrus juices. Today, it is most associated with Peru, which even has a holiday to celebrate the dish (June 28, if you're interested). Spaniards arriving in the Americas found that the pre-Inca peoples of Mocha had a similar dish, which used the fermented juices of the banana passionfruit. There is archeological evidence of ceviche's consumption as far back as 2,000 years ago.

Because undercooked seafood can carry pathogens, it's important to use fresh shrimp in this recipe. It may be safer to use blast-frozen shrimp, as the process kills some parasites.

SERVES: 4 AS AN APPETIZER

PREP TIME: 10 MINUTES

COOKING TIME: 45 MINUTES

1 RED ONION, FINELY CHOPPED

1/2 LB. SHRIMP, PEELED, CHOPPED INTO 1/2" PIECES

1 CUP LIME JUICE

1 SMALL (LEBANESE OR PERSIAN) CUCUMBER, PEELED, SEEDED, AND FINELY DICED

2 TOMATOES, SEEDED AND FINELY DICED

1/2 BUNCH FRESH CILANTRO, CHOPPED

1 TSP. TABASCO (OR TO TASTE)

SALT TO TASTE

1. Soak the chopped onion in ice water for 5 minutes to reduce the astringency, then drain well and set aside. Place the chopped shrimp in a nonreactive bowl, then add the lime juice and onion. Mix well, cover, and refrigerate for at least 40 minutes or until the shrimp turns opaque and appears cooked.

2. Drain all but ¼ cup of the lime juice, then add the cucumber, tomatoes, cilantro, Tabasco, and salt to taste. Serve with Tostones (page 118) and Guacamole (56).

Seafood Paella

SERVES: 4

PREP TIME: 20 MINUTES

COOKING TIME: 1 HOUR

Paella is a dish from Valencia, along Spain's eastern coast. Rice was a product of Moorish influence and was a staple in Spain by the 15th century. Paella developed over the years as people began to add combinations of meats and vegetables. While water vole was one of the first meats used in paella, today's Valencian paella includes rabbit, chicken, snails, and beans; seafood paella is equally popular and is considered a traditional dish along the Valencian coast.

Using an appropriate type of rice is important, as many varieties were specially bred to absorb liquid without losing texture. Calasparra and bomba rices are preferred and are available from gourmet food suppliers and online. Arborio, a common risotto rice, fares pretty well. In a pinch, plain calrose rice will get the job done.

Paella is best made over an open flame and is traditionally prepared outdoors.

---

3 CUPS CHICKEN STOCK (PAGE 42)

1 PINCH SAFFRON THREADS (ABOUT 10 STRANDS)

1 TBSP. OLIVE OIL OR GHEE

1 CHORIZO SAUSAGE, SLICED

1 ONION, FINELY CHOPPED

1 RED BELL PEPPER, DICED

1 GREEN BELL PEPPER, DICED

3 CLOVES GARLIC, MINCED

1 1/2 CUPS CALASPARRA OR BOMBA RICE (ARBORIO OR CALROSE IS OKAY)

2 MEDIUM TOMATOES, SEEDED AND COARSELY CHOPPED

1/2 CUP FROZEN PEAS

3 BAY LEAVES

SALT AND BLACK PEPPER TO TASTE

1/2 LB. SHELL-ON SHRIMP (8-10)

1/4 LB. LIVE MUSSELS (10-15)

1/2 LB. LIVE CLAMS (10-15)

1 SMALL HANDFUL FRESH PARSLEY, CHOPPED

LEMON WEDGES FOR SERVING

1. In a small pot, bring the chicken stock to a boil on high heat. Add the saffron and remove from the heat, allowing the flavors to infuse for at least 10 minutes. In the meantime, start your paella.

2. In a paella pan or large skillet, heat the olive oil or ghee on medium heat. Add the chorizo and sauté until browned, about 2 minutes. Add the onion and bell peppers and sauté until softened, about 6 minutes, stirring occasionally. Add the garlic and sauté for another minute, then add the rice. Toast until the rice is opaque, about 4 minutes, stirring often. Add the tomatoes, peas, saffron-infused stock, and bay leaves and gently stir until well mixed. Season with salt and pepper to taste. Bring to a boil, then reduce the heat to low. Allow to simmer without stirring until most of the liquid has been absorbed, about 15 minutes.

3. Arrange the shrimp, mussels, and clams on top of the paella, then loosely cover with a lid or foil and simmer for another 10 minutes or until the mollusks have opened and the shrimp has turned pink. The mollusks will add liquid to the paella as they open, so remove the lid and reduce the liquid for 2 minutes before serving. Stir in the parsley and serve with lemon wedges.

Crawfish Étouffée

Étouffée is a Cajun dish in which a main ingredient (usually shellfish) is smothered in a chunky sauce made of stock, tomatoes, peppers, and onions. Crawfish is the most popular version of étouffée; shrimp is easier to find and equally delicious.

As mentioned in my Dirty Rice recipe (page 100), Cajun cuisine comes from Acadian immigrants deported from Canada to Louisiana in the 18th century who brought French culinary techniques to locally available ingredients. Crawfish étouffée is a prime example of a perfect pairing of the two cultures. Serve it with white rice (page 96) or Cauliflower Rice (page 78).

Given the number of ingredients in this dish, make sure to chop your vegetables and portion out your spices ahead of time.

SERVES: 4

PREP TIME: 20 MINUTES

COOKING TIME: 25 MINUTES

6 OZ. BACON (6 SLICES), CHOPPED

2 TBSP. BUTTER

1 ONION, FINELY CHOPPED

2 STALKS CELERY, FINELY CHOPPED

1 RED OR GREEN BELL PEPPER, FINELY CHOPPED

1 TOMATO, CHOPPED

1 SHALLOT, MINCED

4 CLOVES GARLIC, MINCED

1 TSP. PAPRIKA

1/2 TSP. CAYENNE PEPPER

1/2 TSP. DRIED THYME

1/2 TSP. DRIED OREGANO

3 BAY LEAVES

1/4 CUP WHITE RICE FLOUR

3 CUPS CHICKEN BROTH (PAGE 42)

1/2 TSP. SEA SALT

1/2 TSP. BLACK PEPPER

2 LBS. CRAWFISH TAILS OR RAW SHRIMP

1/4 CUP HEAVY CREAM

2 TSP. WORCESTERSHIRE SAUCE (5 SQUIRTS)

1-2 TBSP. HOT SAUCE, LIKE FRANK'S REDHOT OR TABASCO (5-10 SQUIRTS)

1 SMALL HANDFUL FRESH PARSLEY, CHOPPED

1. In a large skillet, sauté the bacon on medium heat until crispy, about 6 minutes. Add the butter, onion, celery, and bell pepper and simmer until slight softened, about 4 minutes. Add the tomato and shallot and sauté until the tomato softens, another 5 minutes. Add the garlic, paprika, cayenne pepper, thyme, oregano, and bay leaves and sauté until fragrant, about 1 minute.

2. Stir in the flour and continue to sauté until the flour imparts a toasted smell, about 2 minutes. The mixture will be really dry at this point, and some of the flour may start to stick to the skillet, which is fine. Stir in the broth, salt, and pepper and simmer until the sauce thickens and reduces to the consistency of gravy, about 6 minutes.

3. If using crawfish tails, gently stir them in and simmer until warmed through, about 2 minutes. If using shrimp, stir them in and simmer until cooked through, gently stirring occasionally, about 3 minutes. You'll know that the shrimp are fully cooked when they are pink and opaque and start to curl.

4. Remove the heat and stir in the cream, Worcestershire, hot sauce, and most of the parsley. Taste and add more salt and pepper if needed. Serve with white rice or cauliflower rice and extra hot sauce, scattering the remaining parsley on top right before serving.

Grilled Lobster

Lobsters have been caught and enjoyed as a delicacy worldwide throughout history, but the discovery of the American lobster in New England brought a lot of attention its way in the 1800s. Today, twice as many American lobsters are consumed annually as compared to the second most harvested lobster, the Norway lobster.

If you've never cooked a live lobster before, be prepared for the visceral experience of dunking a lobster in boiling water; it's not often that we physically kill an animal with our bare hands, and many home chefs find it unnerving. One pair of recipe testers almost ended the evening with two pet lobsters because they had a hard time serving as executioners.

Freezing the lobsters ahead of time will make them docile, though whether freezing numbs the pain of boiling is a subject of debate. Some chefs like to stab into the lobster's brain before boiling, but since the lobster has several nerve centers, it's widely believed that this technique neither kills the lobster nor renders it unconscious. Meanwhile, some scientists believe that lobsters have such simple nervous systems that they don't feel pain.

While many Western lobster eaters shy away from eating tomalley (also known as "mustard" or guts), it is full of intense, delicious flavor. Adding the tomalley to the butter sauce before grilling the lobsters is an easy way to dramatically increase the tastiness of this dish. If the idea of eating tomalley is unappealing, simply omit it from this recipe.

SERVES: 2
PREP TIME: 10 MINUTES
COOKING TIME: 20 MINUTES

---

2 LIVE LOBSTERS, 1–1 1/2 LBS. EACH

1/4 CUP SALT PER 1 GALLON WATER

6 TBSP. BUTTER

1 TBSP. OLIVE OIL

4 CLOVES GARLIC, COARSELY CHOPPED

1/2 TSP. RED PEPPER FLAKES

JUICE OF 1 LEMON (2 TBSP.)

1 TSP. LEMON ZEST

1 SMALL HANDFUL FRESH PARSLEY, CHOPPED

BLACK PEPPER TO TASTE

1. In your largest stockpot, add enough cold water to fill the pot three-quarters full, adding salt until it tastes like seawater, then bring to a boil. Prepare an ice bath in a large bowl.

2. Place the lobsters in the freezer for 10 minutes before boiling to make them docile. Carefully drop 1 lobster into the boiling water, holding it under the water with a wooden spoon; parboil for 3 minutes, then remove and place in the ice bath to stop the cooking process. Repeat with the second lobster.

3. Heat the butter, olive oil, and garlic in a small saucepan on medium-low until no longer frothy, about 5 minutes.

4. Using a large, sharp knife, slice the lobsters in half lengthwise and either crack or cut slits in the claws. Remove the tomalley and reserve. Remove the butter sauce from the heat and stir in the red pepper flakes, lemon juice and zest, parsley, and tomalley.

5. Grill the lobsters cut side down on direct high heat for 2 minutes, then flip them and generously apply the butter sauce; grill for another 3 minutes or until the lobster meat is opaque. Serve with fresh-ground pepper and any leftover butter sauce.

Chili Mussels

SERVES: 2 AS A MAIN COURSE, 4 AS AN APPETIZER

PREP TIME: 10 MINUTES

COOKING TIME: 10 MINUTES

A popular appetizer in Australia, chili mussels celebrate the multinationality of that beautiful country. Taking cues from Asian and European cuisines, this dish is both comforting and exotic with its use of wine, tomato sauce, and a hot chile pepper. See the notes in my Clams in White Wine Sauce recipe (page 248) about why farm-raised clams and mussels are preferred over wild-caught.

This dish pairs well with Pão de Queijo (page 121) formed into breadsticks to sop up the extra sauce (pictured on page 95).

---

2 LBS. LIVE MUSSELS (~50)

3 CUPS BASIC RED SAUCE (PAGE 53)

1 BIRD'S EYE CHILE, SEEDS AND RIBS REMOVED, MINCED (OR 1 TSP. RED PEPPER FLAKES)

2 TBSP. BUTTER

2 CLOVES GARLIC

1/2 CUP WHITE WINE

1 TSP. CHOPPED FRESH OREGANO (DRIED IS OKAY)

1 LEMON, CUT INTO SLICES

1. Scrub the mussels under cold water, discarding any that are open and do not spring shut when squeezed.

2. In a small saucepan, heat the red sauce on low until warm, about 20 minutes. Stir in the chile or red pepper flakes.

3. Melt the butter in a stockpot on medium heat for 1 minute, then add the garlic and sauté until fragrant, about 1 minute. Add the wine, increase the heat to medium-high, and bring to a simmer, then gently add the mussels using a slotted spoon. Cover and steam, shaking the pot occasionally, until the mussels open, about 7 minutes. Uncover, stir in the red sauce, and gently toss to combine. Garnish with chopped oregano and serve with lemon slices.

Clams in White Wine Sauce
(Palourdes au Vin Blanc)

While clams, wine, and butter are all delicious, the combination of the three is truly divine. This dish, developed in the Provençal region of France, is the quintessential marriage of these rich, decadent flavors. It is equally tasty when prepared with mussels.

Though wild and sustainably caught seafood is generally ideal, it's better to buy farm-raised clams and mussels. They are raised on ropes suspended above the sea floor, which makes them less gritty than wild clams and mussels dredged from the ocean floor. Dredging up wild clams and mussels can also damage the ocean's ecosystem.

This dish pairs well with Pão de Queijo (page 121) that have been shaped into breadsticks (pictured on page 95).

SERVES: 2 AS A MAIN COURSE, 4 AS AN APPETIZER

PREP TIME: 40 MINUTES

COOKING TIME: 20 MINUTES

4-5 LBS. LITTLENECK CLAMS (~50)

6 TBSP. BUTTER, DIVIDED

2 SHALLOTS, FINELY CHOPPED

6 CLOVES GARLIC, MINCED

1 CUP WHITE WINE

2 BAY LEAVES

1/3 CUP HEAVY CREAM

2 TBSP. CHOPPED FRESH PARSLEY

1/4 TSP. BLACK PEPPER

1. Scrub the clams with a stiff brush and rinse thoroughly under cold water. Soak in cold water for 30 minutes, then drain and rinse again.

2. In a stockpot, melt 2 Tbsp. of the butter on medium heat for 1 minute. Add the shallots and sauté until softened, about 3 minutes. Add the garlic and sauté for another 30 seconds, then add the wine and bay leaves, reduce the heat to medium-low, and simmer for 5 minutes to allow the flavors to marry.

3. Gently place the clams in the stockpot with a slotted spoon. Cover and steam on high heat until the clams open, 5-8 minutes. Remove from the heat. Keeping as much wine sauce in the stockpot as possible, take out the clams with tongs, place in a large bowl, and set aside. Add the cream, parsley, pepper, and the remaining 4 Tbsp. butter to the wine sauce and simmer over medium heat until the butter has melted, about 2 minutes, stirring constantly. Pour the sauce over the clams and serve.

New England Clambake

Clambakes have been prepared along the New England coast for hundreds of years, usually by heating stones in a fire, placing seafood over the rocks using layers of seaweed, and leaving the food to steam for several hours. Since beach fires are increasingly prohibited, many chefs have taken to re-creating clambakes in large pots at home, to the point that this method has become the norm.

This dish typically includes corn on the cob, but I've found that sautéed squash adds the same touch of sweetness without the dubious nutritional profile of corn. Adding steamed artichokes to the meal adds another flavorful dynamic.

SERVES: 6

PREP TIME: 40 MINUTES

COOKING TIME: 45 MINUTES

4 LBS. LIVE CLAMS (~50)

JUICE OF 1 LEMON

4 ARTICHOKES

1 TBSP. OLD BAY SEASONING

1/2 TBSP. KOSHER SALT

1/2 CUP WHITE WINE

6 SMOKED SAUSAGES, CUT INTO 1 1/2" CHUNKS

8 RED POTATOES, QUARTERED

2 LBS. RAW, SHELL-ON SHRIMP

2 TBSP. BUTTER

2 MEDIUM YELLOW SQUASH, SLICED

2 MEDIUM ZUCCHINI, SLICED

SALT AND BLACK PEPPER TO TASTE

1. Scrub the clams with a stiff brush and rinse thoroughly under cold water. Soak in cold water for 30 minutes, then drain and rinse again.

2. Add 1" water and the lemon juice to a stockpot lined with a steamer basket. Rinse the artichokes, cut ½" off each top, and cut the stems so that they are nearly flush with the bottom edge of the leaves. Place the artichokes in the steamer basket. Bring the water to a boil, cover, and steam until the outer leaves pull easily from the artichokes, about 30 minutes.

3. Combine the Old Bay seasoning and kosher salt. Pour the wine into a large stockpot and line it with the sausages. Loosely wrap the clams in cheesecloth or a thin kitchen towel and place over the sausage. Add the potatoes and sprinkle half of the Old Bay seasoning mixture on top. Add the shrimp and sprinkle with the rest of the seasoning. Steam on high for 20 minutes or until the potatoes are fork-tender and the shrimp is pink and curled.

4. As the other ingredients steam, melt the butter in a large saucepan on medium heat for 1 minute. Add the squash and sauté until slightly softened, about 3 minutes, flipping occasionally. Season with salt and pepper to taste.

5. Serve the seafood, artichokes, and squash directly on the table covered with brown kraft paper or newspaper. Serve with melted butter (mixed with garlic for extra kick) and Mayonnaise (page 50).

Choose Round Artichokes

New England Clam Chowder

Chowder get its name from the French word chaudière *("kettle" or "pot"), which in turn is derived from the Latin* caldᵃria *("cauldron"). There's quite a rivalry between the white, creamy New England clam chowder and the clear, tomato-based Manhattan clam chowder—in fact, a bill was introduced into the Maine legislature in 1939 attempting to make it illegal to add tomatoes to clam chowder.*

It wasn't until the Second Vatican Council in the 1960s that Catholics were permitted to eat meat on Fridays (the abstinence period has been reduced to Lent). To provide a seafood option to Catholics, restaurants across the country served clam chowder on Fridays, and the tradition remains today.

SERVES: 6

PREP TIME: 40 MINUTES

COOKING TIME: 45 MINUTES

5-7 LBS. LIVE CLAMS (~50)

3 CUPS WATER

2 (6.5 OZ.) CANS MINCED CLAMS, JUICE RETAINED

6 OZ. BACON (6 STRIPS) OR SALT PORK, COARSELY CHOPPED

1 MEDIUM ONION, FINELY CHOPPED

2 TBSP. WHITE RICE FLOUR

3 MEDIUM RUSSET POTATOES, PEELED AND CUT INTO 3/4" CUBES

1 BAY LEAF

1 CUP HEAVY CREAM

BLACK PEPPER TO TASTE (~1 TSP.)

1 SMALL HANDFUL FRESH PARSLEY, CHOPPED

1. Scrub the clams with a stiff brush and rinse thoroughly under cold water. Soak in cold water for 30 minutes, then drain and rinse again. Place in a stockpot with 3 cups water and steam on high heat for about 4 minutes or until the clams are just slightly open. With tongs, remove the clams and transfer them to a bowl to cool; pour out and reserve all the liquid from the clams along with the water used to steam them. Once the clams are cool, pry the shells open and remove the clam meat (cut it out with a paring knife if needed). Chop the clams into thirds and mix them with the canned clams. Add the juice from the canned clams to the rest of the reserved liquid.

2. In the same stockpot, sauté the chopped bacon or salt pork on medium heat until crispy, about 6 minutes, then add the onion and sauté until the onion is translucent, about 5 minutes. Stir in the flour and sauté until toasted, about 2 minutes. Add the potatoes, bay leaf, and the reserved clam liquid. (Don't pour in the last of the liquid if it looks gritty.) Simmer on medium-low heat for 15-20 minutes or until the potatoes are tender. Do not overcook.

3. Remove the bay leaf and stir in the cream and clam meat. Bring to a simmer and simmer for 2 minutes, stirring often. Add pepper to taste, and salt if needed. Stir in the parsley and serve.

Chesapeake Bay Crab Cakes

Crab cakes originated in colonial America and are still most prevalent in the Chesapeake region, especially Maryland. Today, you can commonly find two types in Maryland: boardwalk crab cakes (fried and served in buns) and restaurant crab cakes (broiled or fried and served on open-faced sandwiches or on their own). These crab cakes embody the Maryland restaurant cakes my family has come to love during our time living in the Baltimore area—with no fillers other than a few ingredients to accent the crab and keep it all together. This is a crab lover's crab cake.

SERVES: 4
PREP TIME: 35 MINUTES
COOKING TIME: 20 MINUTES

1 TBSP. ALMOND MEAL

1 TBSP. COCONUT FLOUR

5 TBSP. MAYONNAISE (PAGE 50)

1 EGG YOLK

2 TSP. WORCESTERSHIRE SAUCE

1 1/2 TSP. OLD BAY SEASONING, PLUS EXTRA FOR SERVING

1 TSP. YELLOW MUSTARD

1 TSP. LEMON JUICE

1 LB. JUMBO LUMP BLUE CRAB MEAT (DUNGENESS IS OKAY), DRAINED

1 LEMON, CUT INTO SLICES

1. In a large bowl, combine all the ingredients but the crab meat and lemon slices. Gently mix in the crab with your hands, then form into 4 baseball-sized balls. Put the cakes on a baking sheet and refrigerate for 30 minutes to help retain their round shape.

2. Rearrange your oven racks so that one rack is near the top of the oven. Preheat the oven to 425°F, then set the oven to broil. Place the crab cakes on the top rack and broil for 5 minutes or until the tops start to turn brown and crispy. Reset the temperature to 425°F and bake for 10 minutes or until the internal temperature of the crab cakes reaches 160°F. Serve with lemon slices and extra pinches of Old Bay seasoning.

Nabemono

Nabemono, also known simply as nabe, is a Japanese hot pot stew. Guests cook the ingredients in a stoneware pot on the dining table using a portable stove. It's a fun way to eat a variety of foods, and each person can tailor their bowl to suit their tastes. While the dish consists mainly of vegetables, seafood is commonly included; thinly sliced beef works as well. It is traditionally cooked in a stoneware pot, but a saucepan can also be used. As long as the food tastes good, your guests won't mind.

There are several different forms of nabe. Chankonabe is typically made with huge quantities of chicken, fish, tofu, and cabbage; sumo wrestlers eat it to gain weight. Sukiyaki uses thinly sliced beef and is eaten with a raw egg dip. Oden is a winter dish that includes hard-boiled eggs, daikon radish, and fish cakes.

Making your own soup broth (dashi) for this dish is a rewarding experience, and the broth can be used in a variety of dishes (like my Steamed Eggs recipe, page 218). Dashi can be made up to 5 days in advance. Mixing in some homemade Fish Stock (page 42), rice wine, and tamari adds even more complexity to the broth. Feel free to experiment with other ingredients, such as shrimp, Siu Yuk (page 177), rice noodles, potato, daikon radish, or kabocha squash.

SERVES: 4 (VARIES BASED ON INGREDIENTS)

PREP TIME: 1 HOUR (TO MAKE THE DASHI)

COOKING TIME: 20 MINUTES

DASHI:

4 CUPS WATER

12 SQUARE INCHES DRIED KOMBU SEAWEED (ABOUT 1/2 OZ.)

1/2 CUP LOOSELY PACKED KATSUOBUSHI (JAPANESE BONITO FLAKES, FROM SKIPJACK TUNA)

2 CUPS FISH STOCK (PAGE 42)

1/2 CUP JAPANESE RICE WINE (MIRIN OR SAKÉ)

1 TBSP. TAMARI

1 BUNCH CHINESE CABBAGE (BOK CHOY OR CHOY SUM)

1/2 HEAD WON BOK CABBAGE, CUT INTO BITE-SIZED CHUNKS

1-2 LBS. SNOW CRAB LEGS, SEPARATED

10-20 SHIITAKE MUSHROOMS

8 OZ. ENOKI MUSHROOMS

3 CARROTS, SLICED

4 OZ. FISH CAKE (LOOK FOR VARIETIES MADE WITH POTATO STARCH AND WITHOUT MSG OR FOOD DYES)

5 GREEN ONIONS, WHITE PARTS SLICED 1" THICK, GREEN PARTS CHOPPED

1. Add the water and kombu to a saucepan and let the kombu soak for 30 minutes. Place the saucepan over medium heat until it just starts to boil, about 8 minutes, then remove the kombu and set aside. Increase the heat to medium-high and add the katsuobushi once boiling; reduce the heat to low and simmer for 10 minutes. Strain the liquid through a cheesecloth or coffee filter, reserving the katsuobushi. The kombu and katsuobushi can be used once more to make a second batch of dashi (called niban dashi).

2. In a nabe pot or shallow stockpot, combine the dashi, fish stock, rice wine, and tamari and bring to a gentle simmer on medium-low heat. Add the remaining ingredients and cook to your liking, in batches as desired.

CHAPTER 9

FRUITS AND DESSERTS

Banana Ice Cream

SERVES: 2

PREP TIME: 2 MINUTES PLUS
4 HOURS

Humans have been flavoring ice in China for at least 5,000 years; Marco Polo brought flavored ice to Italy in the 13th century; and ice cream as we know it was created in the 17th century. Although nothing beats real, homemade ice cream, I can't resist the simplicity and whole-foods nature of making ice cream out of frozen bananas.

MAPLE WALNUT ICE CREAM

COOKING TIME: 5 MINUTES

1 LB. RIPE BANANAS (3 BANANAS), CUT INTO 2" CHUNKS

1/4 CUP WALNUTS

2 TBSP. MAPLE SYRUP

1. Put the bananas on a baking sheet and freeze until solid, at least 4 hours. Toast the walnuts on medium-low heat for about 5 minutes, then let cool and chop.

2. Add the frozen bananas to a food processor and process, stopping frequently to stir. Add the maple syrup and process to incorporate. When smooth, mix in the walnuts by hand and serve immediately.

PISTACHIO ICE CREAM

1 LB. RIPE BANANAS (3 BANANAS), CUT INTO 2" CHUNKS

1/4 CUP PISTACHIOS, COARSELY CHOPPED

1. Put the bananas on a baking sheet and freeze until solid, at least 4 hours. Add the frozen bananas to a food processor and process, stopping frequently to stir. Add the chopped pistachios and process until smooth; serve immediately.

MOCHA ICE CREAM

COOKING TIME: 5 MINUTES PLUS 1 HOUR TO SET

1 LB. RIPE BANANAS (3 BANANAS), CUT INTO 2" CHUNKS

1/4 CUP COLD STRONG COFFEE

1 TBSP. UNSWEETENED COCOA POWDER

1/2 TSP. VANILLA EXTRACT

2 TBSP. MAPLE SYRUP

1. Put the bananas on a baking sheet freeze until solid, at least 4 hours. Add the frozen bananas to a food processor and process, stopping frequently to stir. Add the coffee, cocoa powder, vanilla, and maple syrup and process to incorporate; remove when smooth. Return to the freezer until it reaches the desired hardness, about 1 hour.

Strawberry Granita

SERVES: 4

PREP TIME: 10 MINUTES

FREEZING TIME: 8 HOURS

2 PINTS STRAWBERRIES, STEMS REMOVED

1 1/2 CUPS APPLE JUICE

1/2 CUP COLD WATER

Granita is a semi-frozen dessert, similar to sorbet, that originated in Sicily and dates back to the Middle Ages. There are many variations of the dish, most associated with the texture; the longer you let the mixture freeze before breaking up the ice crystals, the less smooth it will be. I opted for the coarse version, which is more typical of its Sicilian origin.

1. Blend the strawberries, then strain out and discard any seeds. Combine the strawberry puree, apple juice, and water in a rimmed baking sheet. Place the baking sheet in the freezer and freeze for 4 hours. Use a fork to break up the ice crystals, then return to the freezer.

2. Repeat this process 2 more times, breaking up the ice crystals every 2 hours for a total of 8 hours of freezing time. Serve cold.

Almond Panna Cotta

SERVES: 4

PREP TIME: 5 MINUTES, PLUS 4 HOURS TO SET

COOKING TIME: 20 MINUTES

Panna cotta is an Italian desert of unknown origin. Traditional recipes called for boiling fish bones to extract the collagen necessary to thicken this dish; today, gelatin powder is used. Panna cotta is often made with cream and milk, but almond milk variations like this one are also popular.

2 CUPS UNSWEETENED ALMOND MILK

3 TBSP. HONEY

1 VANILLA BEAN, SPLIT (OR 1 TSP. VANILLA EXTRACT)

2 TBSP. HOT WATER

1 1/2 TSP. GELATIN POWDER

1. In a saucepan, combine the almond milk, honey, and vanilla bean (including its seeds). Bring to a simmer on medium-low heat, stirring frequently to dissolve the honey. Once simmering, remove from the heat and let sit for 5 minutes.

2. In a separate bowl, combine the hot water and gelatin, whisking with a fork until the gelatin dissolves. Pour into the almond milk mixture. If you used a vanilla bean, strain and discard the bean and seeds. Divide into 4 small bowls, glasses, or jars and refrigerate until set, about 4 hours. Serve with fresh fruit or berries.

3. Feel free to experiment with the flavors of panna cotta. One friend steeped a spiced tea bag in the almond milk as it simmered, which added some kick. Alternatively, you could add and melt 2 oz. dark chocolate as you finish simmering the almond milk. A traditional panna cotta is slightly less thick than custard; for a thicker variation, increase the amount of gelatin to 2 Tbsp.

Chocolate Pudding

The etymology behind the word pudding *is complicated. The first puddings were boiled and were similar to sausages, somewhat like the famous Scottish dish haggis. English puddings were historically either savory or sweet, with meat no longer associated with puddings after the 18th century; modern English puddings are usually savory rolls made from a batter of milk, flour, and eggs, similar to the American popover.*

The American interpretation of pudding is most similar to custard. The Romans first made egg-based custards, which were both sweet and savory. In the Middle Ages, custard transformed into the sweet, pudding-like consistency it's known for today. Sometime in the middle of the 19th century, Americans abandoned the traditional European boiled puddings. At the same time, instant custard powder was invented, which eliminated the need for fresh eggs. By the turn of the 20th century, instant custard, now termed pudding, became extremely popular in United States.

The flavor of this pudding is determined by the chocolate you use; dark chocolate will create a dark pudding. I recommend using a chocolate bar that you enjoy on its own.

There are two ways to make this dish dairy-free. Substituting coconut milk for heavy cream adds tropical notes, and the coconut milk thickens more quickly than cream. You can also use almond milk instead of heavy cream for a more even-flavored substitution, but be sure to double the arrowroot starch to get the right consistency.

SERVES: 6-8

PREP TIME: 20 MINUTES, PLUS 1 HOUR TO SOAK THE DATES AND 1 HOUR TO SET

COOKING TIME: 20 MINUTES

---

2 TBSP. ARROWROOT STARCH

1/4 TSP. SEA SALT

3 CUPS HEAVY CREAM

1/2 CUP WHOLE DATES, SOAKED FOR 1 HOUR AND PURÉED (ADD SOME OF THE SOAKING WATER IF TOO THICK TO PURÉE)

6 OZ. OF YOUR FAVORITE CHOCOLATE BAR, COARSELY CHOPPED

1 TSP. VANILLA EXTRACT

1. In a metal mixing bowl or double boiler, combine the arrowroot starch and salt. Slowly whisk in the cream and continue to whisk until well mixed. Suspend the bowl over a saucepan of simmering water and stir frequently until thickened, about 15-20 minutes. Mix in the dates and chocolate and incorporate until melted, about 2 minutes. Stir in the vanilla and remove from the heat. Pour everything through a mesh strainer into a measuring cup, stirring to help strain; discard any remaining date pulp, then pour the pudding into individual bowls or glasses. Refrigerate for 30 minutes to set.

Rice Pudding

SERVES: 6

PREP TIME: 5 MINUTES

COOKING TIME: 1 HOUR

Rice pudding is an ancient dish, much like Congee (page 106). The rice pudding we are familiar with in Western culture originated in the Roman era and was used as a medicine to settle upset stomachs. Recipes written as far back as 500 years ago bear the same ingredients as the ones listed below.

1/2 CUP SHORT-GRAIN RICE

1 CUP WATER

1 VANILLA BEAN, SPLIT (OR 1 TSP. VANILLA EXTRACT)

1 TSP. LEMON ZEST

1 CUP HEAVY CREAM

1 PINCH SALT

2 TBSP. HONEY, OR TO TASTE

CINNAMON, NUTMEG, OR BERRIES FOR SERVING

1. Rinse the rice until the water runs clear, about 3-4 changes of water, then drain and place in a medium-sized saucepan. Add 1 cup water and let the rice soak for 10 minutes. Cover and bring to a boil over high heat without lifting the lid, which should take about 3 minutes; listen for sounds of water boiling.

2. Once it starts boiling, reduce the heat to low and simmer until the rice starts to make a hissing sound, which indicates that the water has evaporated, about 10-15 minutes. Remove from the heat and let sit, covered, for 5 minutes.

3. Stir in the vanilla bean, lemon zest, cream, and salt; bring to a simmer on low heat and cook until the rice is tender, 10-15 minutes, stirring often to prevent scorching. Add honey to taste, about 2 Tbsp. Remove and discard the vanilla bean. Divide the pudding among 6 serving bowls and top with cinnamon, nutmeg, or berries. Serve hot or chilled.

4. For a more tropical-flavored rice pudding, use coconut milk instead of cream. Almond milk can also be used, although ¾ cup is preferred since it is generally thinner than cream or coconut milk.

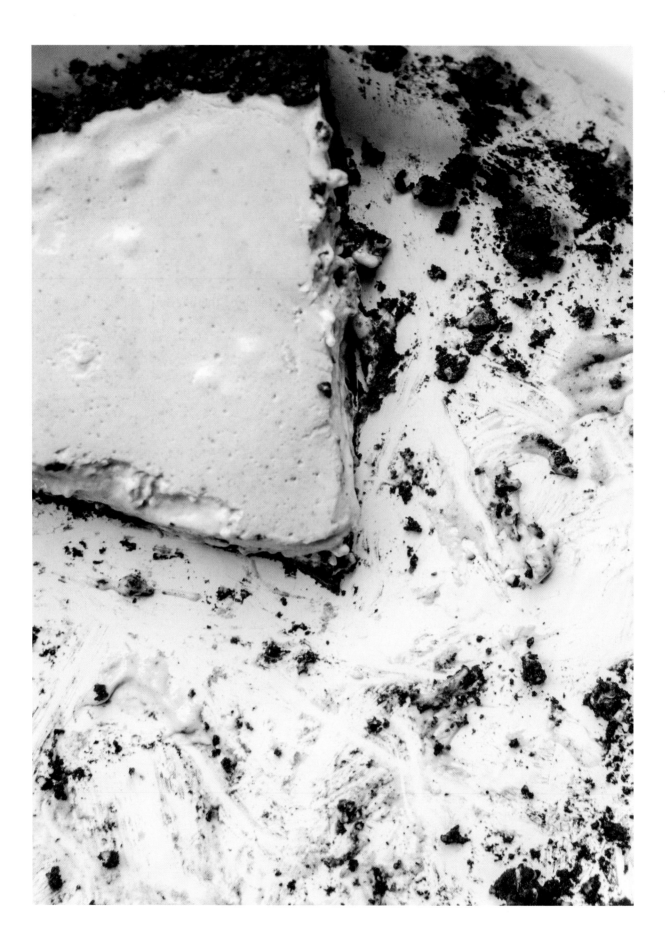

Banana Cream Pie

SERVES: 8

PREP TIME: 2 1/2 HOURS, PLUS 4 HOURS TO SET

COOKING TIME: 30 MINUTES

Banana cream pies can be found in cookbooks dating back to the 19th century, and they hold a special place in the hearts of many who grew up eating them. Cream pies were common even in medieval times, but bananas didn't rise to fame in everyday kitchens until the 19th century. In the 1950s, the United States Armed Services voted the pie their favorite dessert. Today, it usually lags behind apple, pumpkin, and pecan pie in popularity.

In case you were wondering, March 2 is National Banana Cream Pie Day.

CHOCOLATE CRUMB BASE:

1 CUP HAZELNUT FLOUR

1/3 CUP UNSWEETENED COCOA POWDER

1 TBSP. TAPIOCA STARCH

1 TBSP. COCONUT PALM SUGAR

1/4 TSP. BAKING SODA

1 STICK (8 TBSP.) BUTTER, MELTED

1 PINCH SEA SALT

2 TBSP. MAPLE SYRUP

BANANA CREAM FILLING:

2 VERY RIPE BANANAS

1 1/2 CUPS PLUS 2 TBSP. HEAVY CREAM, DIVIDED

3 EGG YOLKS

1 PINCH SALT

1 TBSP. GELATIN POWDER

2 TBSP. BUTTER, CHOPPED

1 TBSP. MAPLE SYRUP

2 JUST-RIPE BANANAS, SLICED

1. Preheat the oven to 325°F. Combine the hazelnut flour, cocoa powder, tapioca starch, coconut palm sugar, baking soda, melted butter, and salt in a bowl. Spread the mixture on a silpat or nonstick baking sheet and bake for 25 minutes or until cooked through. Let cool completely, about 1 hour.

2. Transfer the cookie to a large mixing bowl. With a spoon, break the cookie apart to a coarse crumb. Stir in the maple syrup to bring the mixture together. Press evenly into the base and sides of a pie dish and refrigerate until chilled, about 1 hour.

3. To make the banana cream filling, place the very ripe bananas, ½ cup of the cream, egg yolks, and salt in a blender. Blend until smooth, then transfer to a saucepan. Warm over medium-low heat, stirring constantly with a spatula; remove from the heat as soon as it comes to a boil, 10-15 minutes.

4. In a small bowl, mix together 2 Tbsp. of the cream and the gelatin, then add to the banana mixture. Set aside and allow to cool for 15 minutes.

5. Whisk the remaining 1 cup cream to soft peaks, then fold in the banana mixture. Pour half of the banana cream into the pie shell, cover it with a layer of sliced bananas, and top with the remaining banana cream. Refrigerate until set, about 4 hours.

Birthday Cake

Cakes have been an integral part of human civilization for thousands of years, as evidenced by their historical use in ceremonial occasions like weddings and birthdays. Birthday cakes in particular date back to the Roman era and have endured as an integral part of western European tradition ever since. Germans came up with the idea of adding candles in the 1700s.

Chestnut flour is an excellent baking flour, but somewhat uncommon in everyday grocery stores. The fact that it's hard to find lends credence to the idea that cakes should be reserved for special occasions. As we like to say at my house, this is an everyday cake, but not an every day cake. Chestnut flour is sold online, usually imported from Italy. To make a chocolate cake, replace the rice flour with ¼ cup cocoa powder.

SERVES: 8
PREP TIME: 10 MINUTES
COOKING TIME: 1 HOUR

3/4 CUP CHESTNUT FLOUR

1/3 CUP TAPIOCA STARCH

1/3 CUP POTATO STARCH

1/4 CUP RICE FLOUR

1/2 TSP. BAKING SODA

2 PINCHES SALT, DIVIDED

1/2 CUP BUTTER, ROOM TEMPERATURE

1/2 CUP COCONUT PALM SUGAR

4 EGGS, ROOM TEMPERATURE, SEPARATED

1 TSP. VANILLA EXTRACT

1 CUP HEAVY CREAM

MAPLE BUTTERCREAM (BELOW)

1. Preheat the oven to 325°F. In a bowl, combine the chestnut flour, starches, rice flour, baking soda, and a pinch of salt, then set aside.

2. In a separate mixing bowl, beat the butter and sugar with an electric or stand mixer until pale and fluffy, 3-4 minutes. Add the egg yolks one at a time while the mixer is running, then add the vanilla. Beat in the flour mixture and the cream in batches, starting with a third of the flour followed by half of the cream.

3. In a separate, smaller mixing bowl, whisk the egg whites with a pinch of salt until stiff peaks form. Add a spoonful of egg whites to the cake batter to loosen, then fold in the rest with a spatula. Pour the batter into a greased cake pan and bake for 40 minutes. If you want to make a layered cake like in the picture, use two 5" cake pans; otherwise, an 8" pan will work fine for a single-layer cake. To test for doneness, lightly press the top of the cake with your fingers, touching lightly and quickly so as to not deflate or puncture the surface. If it is firm, it's ready; if it gives under slight pressure, it needs more time in the oven.

4. Allow it to cool in the cake pan on a wire rack for 15 minutes before inverting onto a wire rack to cool completely, about 1 hour. Frost the cake with Maple Buttercream.

MAPLE BUTTERCREAM

1 CUP HIGH-QUALITY MAPLE SYRUP

3 EGG YOLKS

1 CUP BUTTER, CUT INTO CUBES

1. Pour the maple syrup into a small saucepan and heat on medium, without stirring, to 240°F, about 15 minutes, swirling the pan occasionally.

2. When the maple syrup is nearly done, beat the egg yolks with the whisk attachment of an electric or stand mixer until pale and fluffy, about 5 minutes.

3. With the egg yolks still inside, turn your mixer on at a slow speed and slowly pour the syrup down the side of the bowl, mixing until incorporated. Continue to mix for another 5 minutes as it comes to room temperature, then add the cold butter in pieces and mix until incorporated.

ENDNOTES AND INDEX

Substitution Guide

Although I believe that certain forms of rice, potatoes, and dairy have a place on an ancestral table (see pages 25-29 for more info), I acknowledge that some people prefer to omit these ingredients from their diet. Below is a guide that shows you how to make easy adjustments to each recipe so that they better fit a more stringent interpretation of the Paleo diet.

Some universal adjustments:

- Ghee can be used in place of butter and is considered Paleo-friendly (it's even Whole30 approved); coconut oil generally can be used if you are looking to go 100% dairy-free.

- Coconut aminos can be used in place of tamari.

- For dishes that are served with rice (like curry), use cauliflower rice.

- Replace green peas with snow or sugar snap peas, or omit them completely.

- I didn't provide substitutions for the honey, maple syrup, and coconut palm sugar found in my recipes. The amounts used are very small, and I feel that removing them would be disruptive to the overall taste of each recipe.

- I also didn't provide substitutions for the wine used in my recipes, as wine is also integral to the flavor of each recipe. If you are concerned about the alcohol content, consider buying a non-alcoholic wine.

SAUCES, CONDIMENTS, AND OTHER BASICS

RENDERED FAT BASICS	No adjustments needed.
STOCK AND BROTH BASICS	No adjustments needed.
GRAVY BASICS	Use coconut flour instead of rice flour in roux-based gravy.
BARBECUE RUBS	No adjustments needed.
BARBECUE SAUCE	No adjustments needed.
MAYONNAISE	No adjustments needed.
BASIC RED SAUCE	No adjustments needed.
SIMPLE BASIL PESTO	Substitute 1 Tbsp. each nutritional yeast and soaked cashews for the cheese.
GUACAMOLE	No adjustments needed.
HARISSA	No adjustments needed.
PRESERVED LEMONS	No adjustments needed.
SATAY SAUCE	No adjustments needed.
TERIYAKI SAUCE	No adjustments needed.

VEGETABLES

GARLIC DILL PICKLES	No adjustments needed.
KABEES EL LIFT (PICKLED TURNIPS)	No adjustments needed.
DO CHUA (VIETNAMESE PICKLED DAIKON AND CARROTS)	No adjustments needed.
KIMCHI	No adjustments needed.
WEDGE SALAD	Use an oil-and-vinegar-based salad dressing.
BEET SALAD (VINEGRET)	Omit the potatoes.
CAULIFLOWER RICE	No adjustments needed.
BIBIMBAP	Serve on a bed of lettuce or over cauliflower rice instead of rice.
CHINESE GREENS	No adjustments needed.
ROASTED ROOT VEGETABLES	No adjustments needed.
ONION RINGS	No adjustments needed.
SAAG PANEER	Omit the paneer cheese.
CREAM OF MUSHROOM SOUP	Use almond milk or coconut milk instead of cream.
FRENCH ONION SOUP	Omit the cheese.

STARCHES

BASIC RICE RECIPES	Cannot be adjusted. Make cauliflower rice instead.
STICKY RICE	Cannot be adjusted. Make cauliflower rice instead.
DIRTY RICE	Make everything but the rice, then toss with cauliflower rice near the end. Use only a little broth.
MEXICAN RICE	Make everything but the rice, then toss with cauliflower rice near the end. Use only a little broth.
FRIED RICE	Make everything but the rice, then toss with cauliflower rice near the end.

CONGEE	Omit the rice to make a thin, nutritious soup.
GARLIC MASHED POTATOES	Use other root vegetables—parsnip, turnip, rutabaga, or a combination. Make with broth instead of cream.
COLCANNON	Use other root vegetables—parsnip, turnip, rutabaga, or a combination. Make with broth instead of cream.
GNOCCHI	Cannot be adjusted.
SWEET POTATO POI (POI 'UALA)	No adjustments needed.
PARSNIP PUREE	No adjustments needed.
TOSTONES	No adjustments needed.
PÃO DE QUEIJO (BRAZILIAN CHEESE BUNS)	Use coconut milk instead of cream and water, and substitute 2 Tbsp. nutritional yeast and extra tapioca starch for the cheese.
PIZZA	Use coconut milk instead of cream and water, and substitute 2 Tbsp. nutritional yeast and extra tapioca starch for the cheese. Top with meats and veggies instead of cheese.

RED MEAT

HEARTY STEW	Omit the potatoes, or substitute turnip or rutabaga.
EYE OF ROUND ROAST	No adjustments needed.
SHEPHERD'S PIE	Top with mashed cauliflower, turnip, rutabaga, or a combination, or parsnip puree.
SALISBURY STEAK	Omit the cream from the broth.
CHICKEN-FRIED STEAK	Dredge in coconut flour instead of rice flour. Make the gravy with coconut flour and omit the cream.
CHILI CON CARNE	No adjustments needed.
BARBECUE BRISKET	No adjustments needed.
STUFFED CABBAGE ROLLS	Use cauliflower rice instead of white rice.
BORSCHT	Omit the potatoes and serve without sour cream.
SWEDISH MEATBALLS (KÖTTBULLAR)	Use coconut milk instead of cream when forming the meatballs. Use coconut flour instead of rice flour and omit the cream when making the gravy.
KALBI (KOREAN SHORT RIBS)	No adjustments needed.
JAPCHAE	No adjustments needed.
JAPANESE BEEF CURRY	Omit the potatoes and use coconut flour instead of rice flour.
LOCO MOCO	Use cauliflower rice instead of white rice.
BEEF RENDANG	No adjustments needed.
PHO	Use a vegetable spiralizer to make zucchini noodles, or use sweet potato noodles.
SUKUMA WIKI	No adjustments needed.
LAMB TAGINE	Serve without yogurt.
ROGAN JOSH (KASHMIRI LAMB CURRY)	No adjustments needed.
SHASHLIK (RUSSIAN SHISH KABOBS)	No adjustments needed.

PORK

BARBECUE PULLED PORK	No adjustments needed.
BARBECUE RIBS	No adjustments needed.
MEATY COLLARD GREENS	No adjustments needed.
PORK ADOBO	No adjustments needed.
SIU YUK (ROASTED PORK BELLY)	No adjustments needed.
LEMONGRASS PORK CHOPS	No adjustments needed.
KALUA PIG	No adjustments needed.
GAMJATANG (PORK NECK SOUP)	Omit the potato.
LECHON ASADO (CUBAN ROASTED PORK)	No adjustments needed.
JERK PORK	No adjustments needed.

POULTRY AND EGGS

ROASTED CHICKEN	No adjustments needed.
COQ AU VIN	No adjustments needed.
SOUTHERN FRIED CHICKEN	Skip the buttermilk step, or use coconut milk instead. Use arrowroot starch instead of potato starch.
TANDOORI CHICKEN	Use coconut milk instead of yogurt, and add an extra 1 Tbsp. lemon juice to the marinade.
BUTTER CHICKEN (MURGH MAKHANI)	Omit the cream.
CHICKEN PAD SEE EW	Use a vegetable spiralizer to make zucchini noodles, or use sweet potato noodles.
CHICKEN PANANG	No adjustments needed.
CHICKEN SATAY	No adjustments needed.
TERIYAKI CHICKEN	No adjustments needed.
YAKITORI	No adjustments needed.
ROASTED DUCK AND POTATOES	Use other root vegetables (beets, parsnips, turnips, or rutabaga) instead of potatoes.
SMOKED TURKEY LEGS	No adjustments needed.
SEPHARDIC JEWISH-STYLE ROASTED EGGS (HUEVOS HAMINADOS)	No adjustments needed.
SHAKSHOUKA	Omit the yogurt.
STEAMED EGGS (GAERAN JIM)	No adjustments needed.
SON-IN-LAW EGGS	No adjustments needed.

SEAFOOD

PESCE AL SALE (SALT-CRUSTED FISH)	No adjustments needed.
CHINESE STEAMED SEA BASS	No adjustments needed.
SOLE MEUNIÈRE	No adjustments needed.
BLACKENED FISH	No adjustments needed.
FISH PIE	Cannot be adjusted—dairy and potatoes are integral parts of this dish.

LOMI LOMI SALMON	No adjustments needed.
CALDO DE CAMARÓN (MEXICAN SHRIMP SOUP)	No adjustments needed.
SHRIMP CEVICHE	No adjustments needed.
SEAFOOD PAELLA	Make everything but the rice, then toss with cauliflower rice near the end. Use only a little broth.
CRAWFISH ÉTOUFÉE	Use coconut flour instead of white rice flour.
GRILLED LOBSTER	No adjustments needed.
CHILI MUSSELS	No adjustments needed.
CLAMS IN WHITE WINE SAUCE (PALOURDES AU VIN BLANC)	Omit the cream.
NEW ENGLAND CLAMBAKE	Omit the red potatoes.
NEW ENGLAND CLAM CHOWDER	Omit the rice flour, cream, and potatoes to make a thin, clear chowder that is still delicious.
CHESAPEAKE BAY CRAB CAKES	No adjustments needed.
NABEMONO	No adjustments needed.

FRUITS / DESSERTS

BANANA ICE CREAM	No adjustments needed.
STRAWBERRY GRANITA	No adjustments needed.
ALMOND PANNA COTTA	No adjustments needed.
CHOCOLATE PUDDING	Use coconut milk or almond milk instead of cream (see notes in recipe).
RICE PUDDING	Cannot be made without rice, but dairy-free options are provided at the bottom of the recipe.
BANANA CREAM PIE	Use coconut milk instead of cream.
BIRTHDAY CAKE	Cannot be adjusted. Consult *The Paleo Chocolate Lover's Cookbook* by Kelly V. Brozyna for some incredible cake recipes.

Acknowledgments

Above all, thanks to my wife, Janey, and son, Oliver. Janey, you've been my rock through this whole process and my partner on this wild ride. Thank you for your support, strength, and love through a very dramatic decade. Ollie, you'll be old enough to read this soon enough: thanks for understanding and having patience when I was busy typing away on the computer and fiddling around in the kitchen, and not putting together Star Wars LEGOs with you. On the bright side, Mom got pretty good at putting them together. I love you guys.

To my friends and family, thanks for your help, encouragement, and feedback as I worked on this project. Mom and Dad (both Crandall and Nagai), brothers and sisters on both sides, thanks for believing in me. To my Navy family, thanks for your unconditional support and for keeping me honest as I continue to juggle two completely different worlds.

Thanks to the people who helped turn this book into a reality. U.S. Wellness Meats and Lava Lake Lamb are awesome and supplied the majority of meats used in these shots. Alex Boake did an incredible job with the food illustrations in this book, knocking them out like a champ and in record time; your true talent brought this book up a big notch in terms of character and presentation. Jeremy Stahl at Sea Dog Barbecue is the reason my grilling and smoking recipes are worth a damn. Also, thanks to the team of recipe testers and editors who helped me tweak everything to make sure I didn't miss anything. Thanks to Victory Belt for your patience, professionalism, and open-mindedness with some of my unconventional design requests, and for walking me through the fun that is writing and releasing a debut cookbook.

To my readers and fellow bloggers, thanks for your continued support and sense of community. Special thanks to my friends in Highbrow Paleo for helping me find and keep my bearing in the muddy waters of food blogging. Michelle and Henry, Diana, Stacy and Matt, Bill and Hayley, Joshua, Melissa, and Brent and Heather—you guys are awesome Paleo friends and cohorts; you've helped challenge me to make the best food possible, just to catch up to you guys.

Big shout-out to Paul Jaminet. I stumbled upon your site in 2010 when I was trying to find some way to justify the fact that I really wanted to eat white rice again! Little did I know that the Perfect Health Diet would form my dietary foundation, keep me engaged in the latest science, and encourage me to tweak and refine my own health choices. Co-presenting with you at AHS 2013 was surreal, but having your name on the front of my first cookbook, not to mention your awesome and perfectly crafted foreword within, is just about the coolest thing ever.

Finally, huge thanks to my dear friend Giang, who helped me design every aspect of this book and either shot or was there to help me shoot nearly every picture. Your critical eye, enthusiasm, and dedication are unmatched, and this book proves it. Thanks for slumming it in the suburbs of Baltimore with us for a whole month last year when you could have been having a lot more fun in London.

Recipe Credits

I consulted a number of cookbooks when crafting this book. While all the dishes in this book are traditional and have origins that are hard to trace, some methods definitely inspired my recipes and deserve mention.

Barbecue Sauce: *Cook's Illustrated*

Beef Rendang: *Cradle of Flavor,* by James Oseland

Chili: *Cook's Illustrated*

Chinese Greens: *Every Grain of Rice,* by Fuchsia Dunlop

Eye of Round Roast: Allrecipes.com

Garlic Dill Pickles: *Wild Fermentation,* by Sandor Ellix Katz

Grilling Tips and Methods: *Cook's Illustrated*

Kimchi: Maangchi Kim (www.maangchi.com)

Lard: *Beyond Bacon,* by Stacy Toth and Matthew McCarry

Maple Buttercream: Martha Stewart (www.marthastewart.com)

Mayonnaise: *Well Fed,* by Melissa Joulwan

Seafood Paella: *Moro,* by Sam and Sam Clark

Swedish Meatballs: *Well Fed 2,* by Melissa Joulwan

Index